COPYRIGHT *for* ADMINISTRATORS

Carol Simpson, JD, EdD
with Christine Weiser, Editor

Professional Development Resources for
K-12 Library Media and Technology Specialists

Library of Congress Cataloging-in-Publication Data

Simpson, Carol, 1949-
  Copyright for administrators / Carol Simpson ; with Christine Weiser, editor.
      p. cm.
  Includes bibliographical references and index.
  ISBN-13: 978-1-58683-323-7 (pbk.)
  ISBN-10: 1-58683-323-5 (pbk.)
  1. Fair use (Copyright)--United States. 2. Copyright--United States. I. Weiser,
Christine. II. Title.
  KF3020.S56 2008
  346.7304'82--dc22

                              2008013973

Cynthia Anderson: Editor
Judi Repman: Consulting Editor

Published by Linworth Publishing, Inc.
3650 Olentangy River Road
Suite 250
Columbus, Ohio 43214

ISBN 13: 978-1-58683-323-7
ISBN 10: 1-58683-323-5

5 4 3 2 1

TABLE *of* CONTENTS

TABLE *of* CONTENTS *continued*

TABLE *of* CONTENTS *continued*

TABLE *of* CONTENTS *continued*

ABOUT *the* AUTHOR

 **CAROL SIMPSON** is Associate Professor (modified service) in the School of Library and Information Sciences at the University of North Texas. She has 25 years of experience in public education, as a teacher, librarian, and district-level administrator. In addition, she holds a law degree, and has worked in the area of school law.

ACKNOWLEDGMENTS

Copyright has become a popular topic (or unpopular, depending on your point of view). While we educators have the idea that we should be able to use anything at no charge because of our altruistic purposes, those who create content have to make a living creating that content we covet. The result is a pair of unhappy partners: the creators who feel that using without paying is the equivalent of stealing, and the users who know that they don't have enough money to provide the resources that students need to meet the achievement society expects. There is no winner in this tug-of-war.

Learning to live with the tension between content creators and content consumers is the goal of this book. And while the target audience for this work is school administrators in general, the inspiration of the content is the cadre of dedicated school librarians who deal in matters of copyright every day. I recommend that any administrator who has additional questions regarding daily practice involving copyright-protected material consult with probably the only staff member with training in that area: the school librarian. To them, I dedicate this book.

I would like to extend my appreciation to my editor, Christine Weiser, my publisher, Marlene Woo-Lun, and stalwart staff members Donna King, Wendy Medvetz, and Ashley Knight. A special word of thanks to Professor Lackland Bloom.

INTRODUCTION

W hether in charge of a building or district, many school administrators have become embroiled in legal tangles over the copy machine or the video recorder. Even worse, administrators who are unprepared may find themselves and their organizations the subject of expensive litigation, costly even if the school is exonerated.

We are in an era characterized by lawsuit. One lawyer, when asked who should be named in a particularly confusing case, is said to have remarked, "Sue 'em all!" Unfortunately, this can be the mindset in copyright litigation. An administrator who is unaware of, or simply chooses to ignore, copyright violations may suddenly find a cease and desist letter on his desk. These letters from attorneys are written in a demanding fashion; violations are spelled out, penalties enumerated, and few options are proposed.

Most school district attorneys are better prepared to deal with civil rights charges than those involving intellectual property. In fact, details of the day-to-day operation of a building or district can seem more pressing than considering the woes of authors and copyright owners. But the fact remains that an administrator who knowingly or unknowingly allows copyright infringement to occur is likely to be named among the defendants in any legal action.

The district will pay for his carelessness. Fines begin at $750 per infringement and rise to $30,000. For "innocent infringers" (those who infringe, but had no reason to think they were infringing), fines are not less than $200, plus attorney's fees. If the infringement is considered willful, penalties can be imposed up to $150,000 per violation per work infringed. In the case of computer software infringements, penalties can be as high as $250,000, and the offense may be considered a felony. The administrator need not actually participate in the infringement to be considered responsible, at least in part, for the violation.

The truth is that most copyright suits are settled out of court. Only a few well-publicized cases have made the trek through the courts to establish the precedents upon which current practice is based. However, even when an infringement action is settled out of court, copyright suits cause stress and cost time and money to resolve the conflict. Copyright watchdog groups use these settled claims as spoils of war to advertise their victories over infringers.

This book can be your primer to the world of copyright, from establishing a copyright policy to supporting the efforts of your most experienced copyright expert, the librarian. This book will help you understand the importance of supporting unequivocal copyright policies, especially in the areas of photocopying, computer software, use of audiovisuals, and the Web.

I've been researching and writing about copyright laws and schools for over 20 years. I started researching my obligations under the law in response to a technological installation. I was astounded at the requirements that I had never learned but which put me and my faculty and administrators at risk. Fortunately, I had a supportive principal and an ethical faculty. All this isn't to say we were always "copyright clean," but we had a building expectation of compliance, we regularly trained our staff, and we monitored our materials and uses with intent to comply with the various laws. Since that time I have continued to read, question, and try to understand. My quest led me to the only place possible to get all the information in the right way—law school. Attending law school gives you a new perspective and appreciation for the law, and its interpretation, and how different courts will view similar sets of facts in totally opposite ways.

The information presented in this volume is not intended to substitute for qualified legal advice, but rather provide a way to help you determine if you need to consult an attorney for detailed guidance on a given situation. If you have any doubt that your activities are within the law, first read the law itself. It is available online from many sites. The suggestions and guidelines contained within this book can help you decide if you are erring on the side of conservatism, or if you might be straying to the hazardous side of the street. If in doubt, consult an attorney—preferably one who specializes in intellectual property (commonly listed as-copyrights, trademarks, and patents-or some combination of those terms). Many copyright attorneys will consult with you for an hour, providing authoritative legal advice, for a few hundred dollars. When dealing with your professional livelihood, two or three hundred dollars is a small sum to pay for a good night's sleep and it can provide enough dependable backup for a firm stand against those who would have you participate in questionable activities.

All these rules and regulations may seem to be too complicated to be worth the trouble. After all, you haven't been caught so far, right? Cease and desist letters are on the rise, and reported cases of schools violating copyright from computer software piracy (Los Angeles Unified School District) to photocopying workbooks (Beaumont, Texas, Independent School District) are only the beginning of the story.

Perhaps a parable will put the whole copyright problem into perspective.

Two second graders are fighting over a ruler. One child is on each end of the ruler, pulling alternately.

"It's mine!" one yells, pulling the ruler.

"No, it's mine!" yells the other, pulling harder in the opposite direction.

The teacher steps in, claiming the disputed ruler. She determines to whom the ruler belongs, turns over the item, and sends him on his way. Taking the other child in tow, she scolds him sternly.

"You don't take what isn't yours without asking first!"

You don't take what isn't yours without asking first.

That's all copyright is about.

Carol Simpson
FALL 2008

HAPTER 1

The Law

It has a name: Title 17, United States Code, Public Law 94-553, 90 Stat. 2541, as amended. Kind of dry sounding, isn't it? Who would guess that this could be one of the most obtuse, complex, and arguably the most hated law affecting schools today? But that is it: U.S. copyright law.

As an administrator, you supervise educators who are using someone else's materials. You need to know something about copyright law and you need to know it quickly. Getting to know the law is a matter of a few key concepts. Once you have those in mind, they apply somewhat uniformly to just about any situation you might encounter.

From the first U.S. copyright law signed by George Washington in 1790, to the current iteration passed in 1976 and tweaked almost annually since, copyright has had a significant impact on the United States. But knowing what happened before is only useful in obtuse cases dealing with old material. For most school employees, 99.999 percent of their copyright questions can be addressed by the current law. So what you need to know is: What does a copyright owner own, and what must I and those I supervise exercise caution in using?

Rights of a copyright holder

The six rights that a copyright owner owns are the rights of:

- Reproduction
- Adaptation
- Distribution
- Public performance
- Public display
- Digital transmission of sound recordings

Knowing what a copyright owner owns is key to understanding how to interpret most copyright situations.

Reproduction

The right of reproduction is the fundamental right of copyright, and was the initial impetus for the law. The copyright owner or his agents control reproduction in all formats. The law specifically mentions various formats when identifying this right by indicating that nonprint reproduction ("phonorecords") is also a right reserved to the copyright holder. Copies need not be exact to be considered reproductions. If you were to make a drawing of Mickey Mouse on a piece of paper, and if such drawing were recognizable as Mickey Mouse, for the purposes of this portion of the law, the drawing would be of Mickey Mouse. Just because a few details have been changed doesn't mean that the use is beyond the restrictions of this right. Making a change in format such as recording a book or digitizing a photo could also be considered to be making a copy or an adaptation or derivative work. An example would be scanning an image for a parent newsletter.

Adaptation

Adaptation is changing a work in some way, or creating a derivative work based on the original. Derivative works are new works created from older, possibly protected works. J. K. Rowling gets paid a lot of money to write books, but she gets paid a lot more when those books are adapted into screenplays and produced as movies or plays. Taking a popular song and writing new words is adaptation. Turning a picture book into a play for the second grade is adaptation. Taking the characters of a book and extending the story is adaptation. Scanning a print work into a digital copy is both reproduction (making a copy) and adaptation (changing the format). The same thing happens when a student modifies the work of an artist to create a new piece of art, or a teacher converts a cartoon into digital format for a PowerPoint presentation. All of these instances create derivative works.

Distribution

When a teacher creates copies of a graphic in a book, the right of reproduction comes into play. When the teacher passes out those copies to her class, the action is affected by the right of distribution. Distribution can occur in many ways. Mailing home newsletters is distribution. Loaning books from the library is distribution. Sending video around the building using the video distribution system is distribution. Putting computer software on the campus network is distribution. Forwarding an email is distribution. Putting student work on the Web is distribution to the world.

If the right of distribution were absolute, you couldn't give a book to your niece for Christmas, nor could you have a yard sale. Loaning books from the library would be a violation of the author's right of distribution as well. So how can we do all of those things and still stay within the law? We rely on a nifty piece of legal doctrine known colloquially as the "right of first sale."

Before we can understand the first sale doctrine, however, we must understand what one owns when one owns a book, for example. When you purchase a book at the local bookstore, you have purchased paper, ink, binding, and a license to read the words until it wears out. You have not purchased the words themselves, nor the expression of the ideas discussed within. First sale doctrine explains that the right of distribution ceases with an item's first sale, meaning that you can do whatever you wish, physically, with the book. You can wrap it up and give it to your niece; you can rip out the pages and wallpaper your study; you can donate it to the Friends of the Library book sale. You own that one physical (as opposed to intellectual) copy of that book, and the copyright owner can do nothing at all to stop whatever private use you make of that physical copy.

WHAT IS "PUBLIC?"

Key to understanding both public performance and public display is comprehension of the legal definition of the term "public." The law defines a public performance as: to perform or display it at a place open to the public or at any place where a substantial number of persons outside of a normal circle of a family and its social acquaintances is gathered; or to transmit or otherwise communicate a performance or display of the work to the public.

Public performance

The right to perform a work publicly is reserved to a copyright owner. "Performance" indicates a work of film, video, dance, theatre, music, and so on. A work need not be performed in its entirety to be considered "performed." In fact, a posting on the CNI-Copyright email list discussed the amount of a musical work that must be used to be considered significant. One lawyer replied that if the work is recognizable, enough has been performed to be considered "significant." Naturally, disagreements over that amount would abound, which is why we must rely on definitions in court interpretations of "significant," which will be highly fact-specific.

Public display

Like the right of public performance, the right of public display controls works displayed in public places. The copyright owner controls displays outside the home. A display is of something static, such as a painting, photograph, or sculpture. It could also apply to literature if the work were exposed to public viewing, such as on the Internet. Section 109 (c) of the law allows legally acquired copies of artwork to be displayed where that work is located; so you can hang a poster you have purchased, or you can display the books that the library owns, but you can't scan those into a Web page and display them around the world. This limited exception to public display does not carry over into public performances of things like movies, videos, sound recordings or music, and so on.

Digital transmission of sound recordings

The newest of the copyright owner's rights, the right of digital transmission of sound recording, came into being with the enactment of the Digital Millennium Copyright Act. The right is a reaction to the loss of control over sound recordings when they are in digital formats. Users would listen to Internet radio stations that streamed pristine digital recordings, and while listening they would capture the audio files. Users could burn their own CDs of their favorite songs rather than going to the music store to purchase copies. As a result, earnings in the music industry began to decline. Users were getting the music without paying any fees whatsoever.

> *Record companies felt that they should get their share of the profits one way or another. This new right allows them to do just that. These royalties also apply to any audio streamed from school Web sites.*

As a result, based on the number of listeners, Internet radio stations must pay hefty royalties to record companies (the copyright owners) through rights brokering organizations. Such fees are not new. Analog (AM and FM) radio stations have paid licensing fees for many years. However, the mandatory fees imposed on digital transmission were many times higher than those paid by analog stations, primarily because of the ability to copy perfect quality transmissions. Record companies felt that they should get their share of the profits one way or another. This new right allows them to do just that. These royalties also apply to any audio streamed from school Web sites.

MORAL RIGHTS

A new group of rights was granted by Congress in 1990 called "moral rights." These rights apply to certain types of visual artwork (painting, sculpture, etc.) that are produced in limited quantities (fewer than 200). In such cases the author can require that her name remain with the object. In addition, artists have some power to prevent their artworks from being defaced or destroyed. So, if the work was damaged or destroyed, intentionally or unintentionally, the students would have grounds to sue the school for a violation of moral rights. Painting over the work, remodeling the building, or even allowing other students to deface the work with graffiti could be taken as potential causes for action.

> *For example, moral rights would be significant for a school if the school had students paint a mural, or other artwork. The students would own the copyright in the work, and could demand that their names be displayed with the work.*

HOW DOES ONE GET A COPYRIGHT?

In the years up to 1976, authors had to proactively register their works in order to achieve copyright protection. That changed with the enactment of the 1976 copyright law, which protected a work as soon as it was "fixed in tangible form." A work may be fixed by being:

- written on paper
- painted on canvas
- saved to disk
- recorded on tape
- exposed on film
- or any other method that creates a permanent record of the creation

Any creative work that is recorded in such a manner is automatically granted the protection of copyright for the author/creator. However, if one wishes to be able to sue for damages should the copyright be infringed, "timely" registration of the copyright is required. The necessary information on registration of a copyright is available from the Copyright Office in Washington, D.C. (<www.copyright.gov>). Registration requires submission of a number of copies of the work to the Copyright Office, along with a completed form and the necessary fee. The fee varies from time to time and from type of work registered, but typically it is about $45 per work.

Works can be registered as a "collection," so people who write short stories or haiku can rest assured that they won't go broke registering each small item.

WHAT CAN'T BE PROTECTED BY COPYRIGHT?

The following works are not protected by copyright:

- Facts are not protectable. Facts are owned by all mankind, and no one person owns, for example, the multiplication tables, or the list of the ten longest rivers in the world.

- Works that have not been fixed in a tangible medium of expression, such as dance that has not been codified or recorded, or an improvisational speech that has not been transcribed or recorded, cannot be protected by copyright. Recent upheaval about university note-taking services such as <www.cramster.com> have emphasized that course lecture notes are protected by copyright because they are fixed, but the actual delivery of the lecture (unless the notes are read verbatim) is not protected.

- Ideas, procedures, methods, and discoveries are not protectable by copyright (patent covers these), but descriptions or illustrations of these items may be protected by copyright.

- Works containing only non-protected material with no original authorship, such as plain calendars, lists of common facts, charts of measures, and so on are not protected.

- Works created by the U.S. Government are usually not protected by copyright. The prohibition on federal copyright involves works such as those created by members of Congress within their congressional duties, or employees of federal agencies as part of their job responsibilities. Some federally funded projects written by non-federal employees *may* have copyright protection, so it is always wise to investigate the copyright status of any work before making free use of it. The works of state and local governmental agencies may or may not be protected by copyright. Check thoroughly.

WORK FOR HIRE

Now, I will tell you that I have lied to you. While it is true that a copyright vests at the moment of creation, it doesn't always go to the creator. Take, for example, a classroom teacher who creates a series of science worksheets. The worksheets are particularly effective, so the teacher would like to compile the worksheets into a book that she will offer to a publisher. The only catch to this plan is that the teacher's district owns the copyright in the worksheets, barring any contract or agreement that would restrict that arrangement. The reason this is true is that the worksheets were created as part of the teacher's job. This concept is known as "work for hire." Just about anything that a teacher or administrator does within the context of his job could be claimed as the intellectual property of the school. A common question is to inquire if doing the work at home or on weekends or vacation makes any difference in the work-for-hire rules. Actually, no, it makes no difference. If the work was done "within the scope of employment," it matters little where or when the work was done. If the work was for fourth grade science, in this example, the school could make a very good case that the work belonged to them. However, if you are teaching fourth grade science, but write a college physics textbook in your spare time at home, the school would be hard pressed to convince a court that this work was part of your work as a fourth grade science teacher. Check the standard teacher contract if you have questions about your district.

A clause in teacher contracts regarding copyright ownership can forestall later disagreements about who owns material created during a teacher's employment with the district.

DURATION OF COPYRIGHT

What follows are rules regarding the duration of copyright for works created after October 27, 1998 (when the Sonny Bono Copyright Term Extension Act went into effect):

- Copyright, as of the publication date of this book, lasts for the life of the author, plus 70 years. If there are two or more authors, the work is protected for the life of the longest lived author, plus 70 years.

- For works of corporate authorship (such as a film where there are dozens of contributors, or a committee report or other internal document of an organization), works for hire and pseudonymous works, copyright protection extends for 95 years from the date a work is published or 120 years from the date it was created, whichever is shorter.

- For works published by a group (the National Education Association, for example) or works of diffuse authorship such as a film (there is a producer, director, actors, editors, musicians, set designers, wardrobe, and makeup who all contribute to the final product) the duration of copyright is 95 years from the date of creation of the work.

- Works published before 1923 are currently in the public domain in the United States. Those created between 1923 and 1978 have varying periods of copyright protection.

- The time of creation (or registration) determines if, and how long, a work is protected. Laura Gasaway, librarian and law professor, has a Web page that explains when works pass out of the protection of copyright at: <http://www.unc.edu/~unclng/public-d.htm>.

How do you know if a work is protected? If a work was created in the United States after January 1, 1978 you know that the work was automatically protected by copyright at the moment it was "fixed." After 1989, there need not be a "C-in-a-circle" mark (©) or other notification of copyright, and the author need not have registered his work with the Copyright Office in order to own a life-plus-70 years copyright on the work. For works created prior to January 1, 1978, a notice of copyright and registration with the Copyright Office were required to obtain valid copyright protection. Those works published without such notice were considered to be in the public domain without formal copyright protection. For unpublished works (such as private letters and diaries, manuscripts, family photos, etc.), however, notice and registration are not required, and the works retained their copyright protection for many years. See Laura Gasaway's chart on her Web page for more detailed information.

The process for registering a copyright is set out by type of material. All require a $45 registration fee (as of this book's publication date), plus some copy of the material being registered. The requirements for the various types of registerable materials can be found online at <http://www.loc.gov/copyright/circs/>.

RECENT LAWS

Copyright hasn't stayed static since the passage of the 1976 revision. In virtually every session of Congress, someone introduces (and often passes) a bill that tweaks copyright law in some fashion. What follows are some of the more important copyright-related laws passed since 1976.

NET Act

The "No Electronic Theft" Act (NET Act), signed into law on December 16, 1997, closed a loophole in earlier criminal law that allowed those who intentionally shared copyrighted computer software via the Internet to be exempt from criminal prosecution if the suspect made no profit on the exchange. Reproduction of copies worth, in total, over $1,000 brings the act into play. Trading software with a total value of more than $1,000 also is covered under this law. The NET Act first declared that reproduction and distribution may be by electronic as well as physical means. (UCLA, 1998; United States Department of Justice, 1998) "Computer software" in this law includes MP3 files, so those who trade illegal digital audio files over the Internet could fall into the criminal category established in this Act.

Visual Artists Rights Act

Passed in 1990, the Visual Artists Rights Act (VARA) puts artists in control of their works in more ways than standard copyright allows. It is significant for those who create derivative works, because the artist has complete control over attribution of his work, even when the physical work has been sold. It is also significant if you have art, even student-produced art, in your school.

The artist has the right to both claim authorship in his work when such attribution has been denied, as well as deny authorship when work has been misattributed or the artist's own work has been changed to the point that the artist feels attribution would be harmful to his reputation. In addition, the artist has the right to prevent the intentional modification of a work, or the destruction of a work of "recognized stature."

Rights granted by VARA exist until the close of the calendar year in which the artist dies, and are not transferable to anyone. Even if the artist sells the physical art and/or the copyright in the art, the artist retains the rights granted by VARA. The rights apply to paintings, drawings, prints, photographs or sculpture, created as unique items or in limited editions of 200 or fewer copies. Certain types of art are specifically excluded from the grant of rights under this act (Hoffman, 2002).

Digital Millennium Copyright Act

Signed into law in October, 1998, the Digital Millennium Copyright Act (DMCA) was opposed from its inception. Library, scientific, and academic groups have long found the provisions of the act to be overbroad and far-reaching.

Basically, the DMCA updated copyright law to account for the Internet and digital technologies. Key provisions included:

- You may not "break" copy protection to copy videos or software to servers, or to make backup copies of videos.

- Libraries and schools **may** crack software to access purchased/licensed software that is not working properly, or to view the list of blocked Web sites in an Internet filter ONLY. These are the two situations that the Register allowed schools to bypass technical protections.

- Schools that provide Internet access can be partially protected from copyright infringement claims if they register an employee as the district's agent with the copyright office and follow a set of procedures in the event of a claim.

- Include the complete copyright notice of the original on copies of protected materials (Lutzker, 1999).

- A computer technician may make a RAM or backup copy of computer software while doing computer hardware repair.

- Libraries and archives can make up to three digital copies of works for preservation purposes (this assumes the works are out of print and in danger of destruction from age or condition), but the works may not be used or distributed outside the premises of the library or archives.

- Schools must pay statutory fees for digital transmission of sound recordings and making the ephemeral copies that are necessary for such transmission (Band, 2001).

- Libraries may migrate works held on obsolete media to current technologies, but the transfers may be made only if you can't buy the same work in a non-obsolete format (Harper, 2001). "Obsolete" means that the hardware to perform or display the work must no longer be available for purchase in the marketplace. (Note that this permission is given to libraries but not to schools or other organizations.)

As you can see, the DMCA created extensive changes in copyright practice as far as digital materials are concerned. Libraries and other groups were not pleased about many of the provisions reported here, and seek modification of the law.

Sonny Bono Copyright Term Extension Act

The Sonny Bono Copyright Term Extension Act (CTEA) went into effect in October, 1998. The Act extended the copyright term of all items under copyright as of the date of the implementation of the Act. Because of the impact of this Act, no published works will enter the public domain until January 1, 2019, at which time all works published in 1923 will enter the public domain.

The Act was heavily opposed by librarians and publishers of public domain works, and publisher Eric Eldred chose to challenge the Act by requesting an injunction. In January 2003, the U.S. Supreme Court ruled that the Act was constitutional, paving the way for its implementation. (*Eldred v. Ashcroft*, 537 U.S. 186, (2003)).

Digital Performance Right in Sound Recordings Act

This Act, passed in 1995, granted the sixth right to copyright holders. The right limits the digital transmission performance of a sound recording. Digital transmission would include Internet transmissions and certain digital satellite transmissions.

TEACH Act

The Technology, Education and Copyright Harmonization Act (TEACH Act) established the rules under which copyright-protected materials could be used in online education. The TEACH Act established a set of criteria that, if followed by schools, would allow the use of limited amounts of copyright protected materials when used in qualifying educational situations.

Individuals with Disabilities Education Improvement Act of 2004

This Act, among other things, established the National Instructional Materials Access Center, whose job is to receive and maintain a catalog of print instructional materials prepared in the National Instructional Materials Accessibility Standard. This collection of print works converted to accessible formats will provide, free of charge, instructional materials for elementary and secondary students who are unable to use standard print materials. Since this free service exists, making local audiovisual copies of print materials (such as recording books onto tape) is an infringement of copyright.

Artists' Rights and Theft Prevention Act of 2005

This Act established criminal penalties for anyone who creates or distributes copies of movies made in theaters with video recording devices, or copies made prior to distribution. Theaters may detain and hold those they catch making copies.

Family Movie Act of 2005

Through a combination of a federal court action and this Act, making copies of copyrighted material in order to remove offensive content is an infringement of copyright. The technology known as Clearplay, which has the ability to watch an unencoded video and block offensive content without making another copy of the original, is acceptable for use in **private households**. Schools are not mentioned in the Act as an acceptable venue for use of this technology. The companies who formerly sold expurgated copies of films have been found guilty of copyright infringement, and all works they sold are infringing copies. *Clean Flicks v. Soderbergh*, 433 F. Supp. 2d 1236 (D.Colo. 2005)

PENALTIES FOR INFRINGEMENT

Should a person choose to ignore the law, the penalty for copyright infringement is not a minor inconvenience. Damages can be actual (true financial damages suffered) or statutory (set by law), depending on how the suit is filed and whether the copyright to the infringed work was registered before the infringement commenced. Statutory fines range from $750 to $30,000 per infringement, with each individual work or event constituting a separate act of infringement. A limited exception permits truly unwary infringers (also called innocent infringers) to have their fines reduced to as little as $200 per work infringed, but such reduction in penalty is at the discretion of the court. To qualify for such an exception, an infringer would have to present a strong case that they truly believed (with reasonable justification) that their use of the work was not infringing. The presence of a copyright notice would, for example, be an excellent reason to believe that an infringement was intentional. If the court decides the infringement was knowledgeable and intentional, statutory damages can run as high as $150,000 per instance. Legal fees and court costs can escalate the true cost of losing a copyright infringement case, since an infringer may be required to pay the copyright holder's attorney's fees and court costs as well as the statutory penalties. To become a criminal offense, 10 illegal copies with a total value of $2,500+ worth of software are all that is required. For complete information about potential penalties and liabilities, see Chapter 5 of U.S. Copyright law at: <http://www.copyright.gov/title17/92chap5.pdf>. See Brad Templeton's "10 Big Myths about Copyright Explained" for more surprising information about copyright: <http://www.templetons.com/brad/copymyths.html>.

> **TIP**
>
> Make sure all of your district hardware that can reproduce includes a notice. The standard notice normally found on photocopiers will work fine. You can find standard stickers at library supply houses, or from <www.AffordableAlternativesInc.com>.

Is there an easily accessible record of suits against schools that one may consult? No. While it is true that court decisions are generally public records, the vast majority of copyright infringement actions are settled out of court. Out of court settlements are between the parties involved, especially when there are no criminal actions involved. The parties may choose to keep the negotiations private, in which case neither party will talk about the events. For that reason, it is difficult to determine how much a school is typically fined for copyright violations. One hears of schools who have been required to purchase legal copies of all software found to be installed illegally, or to purchase a license to show entertainment videos when those had been shown without public performance rights. Other situations may involve punitive fines for illegal reproduction of workbooks or other print materials.

If someone in the district or building violates copyright, that person pays the fine, right? Well, not exactly. Copyright watchdog groups report the results of infringement actions, both as spoils of victory and warnings to potential infringers. Most of the reported cases indicate that the classroom teacher or librarian is only the beginning in naming liable parties. The copyright owner looks for the "deep pockets" in most instances, but when suing schools the copyright owners are more likely to be making a statement or setting a precedent. They want to make an impact on all educators who will hear of the suit.

Many suits go right up the chain of command, from teacher or librarian, to principal, to curriculum director, to superintendent, to the board of education under the assumption that these parties are aware of and responsible for the actions of their employees.

Two supplemental forms of liability enter the picture at this point. School employees can be considered contributory infringers if they assisted or helped the infringer to do the infringing act or if they were in a position to control the use of the copyrighted work. An example of such a situation would be a principal or librarian who loaned two video recorders and a set of patch cords with knowledge that they would be used to copy a copyrighted video. If the principal or librarian is in a position to refuse the loan, but makes the loan anyway while knowing that an infringement will occur, she can be considered a contributory infringer.

Employers would have vicarious liability if they had reason to know an employee was violating copyright and had the power to stop the action but took no action. An example of vicarious liability would be a principal who had been notified that an infringement was taking place but who took no action to stop the theft.

LIABILITY

The teacher's liability–Teachers control many copyrighted works: books, workbooks, video, computer software. Misusing the copyright protected materials puts the teacher at the center of a copyright controversy. The teacher may or may not need assistance to violate copyright, but for the most part the teacher will be the beginning of a chain of copyright liability.

Both vicarious and contributory infringers are just as liable as the person who actually made the copies or used the material.

The technician's liability–Technicians exert control of many aspects of technology. During the course of their jobs, they are aware of certain file transactions, programs installed, and other activities of the network environment. If a technician knows that students (or teachers) are trafficking in illegal materials of any kind, but take no action to stop the activity, they may be found to be complicit.

The librarian's liability–If infringing copies are made on library-owned equipment, the librarian who loaned the equipment could be involved in the infringement action. A case could be made that the librarian knew (or should have known) that the event would be an infringing action. Only with the support of a strong copyright policy, good record keeping, and thorough staff training would the librarian and administrators be able to prove that the infringer was acting as an individual.

The principal's liability–The principal is the instructional and administrative leader in the school. As such, the principal must be aware of curriculum, student issues, staffing and personnel responsibilities, extracurricular activities, equipment and resources, and dozens of other issues affecting the building. With such a vast array of knowledge, it's understandable that when a copyright infringement occurs in a school, the copyright owner will assume that the principal had at least passing knowledge of the event or control over those persons committing the infringement. Such a possibility raises the likelihood that the principal will be named in any potential infringement action against the school.

The superintendent's liability–The superintendent faces a similar situation to a principal. As implementer of board policy, the superintendent has an expectation of supervision of all under her control. While the superintendent will probably not face a contributory infringement suit, vicarious infringement could be a possibility if a court might believe that the superintendent was aware of the infringement and took no steps to stop it.

The board of education's liability–The board will invariably be named in any copyright lawsuit. As the legal agents for the entity, similar to a corporate board of directors, they are responsible for anything that happens within their organization.

As you can see, the technician, librarian, administrator, and board are at some risk from the illegal activities of others. To that end, it is worthwhile to establish and maintain clear and thorough copyright records, develop workable copyright policies, and to inform school personnel and patrons of their obligations under the copyright law. Annual copyright refresher training, with records of attendance for all personnel, is recommended prudent practice.

Administrators should encourage their teachers and librarians to notify them of copyright violations. Apprising an administrator of a legal violation is akin to notifying her of a fire code violation so it may be corrected before the fire inspector arrives for inspection. Forewarned is forearmed.

STATE COPYRIGHT LAWS

Until 1978, both the state and the federal governments could prosecute most copyright infringement cases. When the 17 U.S.C. § 301 came into effect, anything within the scope of copyright became part of the federal jurisdiction. States do retain some laws to protect sales of sound recordings (many of which are not covered in federal copyright protection, although the underlying printed music is) and videos under piracy statutes (USDOJ, 1997).

WHAT'S GOING TO HAPPEN TO US?

A school may find itself in copyright hot water in any of several ways. Most common is to receive a cease and desist letter. Such a letter may be sent from a company or its attorneys, and generally states that the company is aware that you have violated copyright in some manner. The letter usually states what you are alleged to have done, and what demands the company is making for reparation.

It is not a good idea to ignore such a letter. In most cases the letter will demand some response from you by a given date. If the company does not receive a response to their allegations by that date, further legal action may be taken. If you feel that the allegations are unfounded, you should take this opportunity to present your side of the case to the company or other representative of the copyright holder. But don't take such a step without advising your school's legal counsel about any discussions with a potential litigant. One word of caution: copyright courses are not required in most law schools. Your school's counsel may have taken many courses in education law, but none at all in copyright. Urge a consultation with a copyright specialist if you are uncomfortable with the advice your counsel is giving.

Another way a school might find itself in trouble is to have an attorney or process server appear at the school. They may be accompanied by or be represented by the FBI and federal marshals. Situations such as this require immediate attention of your legal counsel. As a rule, such incidents do not occur without cause, and there is generally sufficient evidence that the plaintiff has convinced a federal judge that there is likelihood of wrongdoing on the part of your building or district and that evidence will likely be concealed or destroyed if not seized. This is the most serious of cases.

HOW IS A SCHOOL PROSECUTED?

Schools may be sued for real or actual damages, or they may be sued for the fines set forth within the law. For a school to be sued for real or actual damages, the amount of material used and the possible loss in value (tangible or intangible) to the copyright holder would likely exceed the damages set forth in the law (statutory damages). Attorney's fees and court costs get added to the fine amount in many cases. Because most cases of use in schools don't involve amounts over $30,000, few cases demand actual damages. Cases where schools systematically duplicate workbooks without paying royalties, or have significant amounts of illegal computer software are two types of copyright actions in which actual damages would be more beneficial to the copyright holder.

WHAT IF THERE IS NO TRIAL?

The vast majority of copyright cases (both involving schools and others) are settled out of court. While such a settlement is always a relief to the school, the rest of us are disappointed because a definitive court ruling helps to define the boundaries of copyright. Copyright is an ever-changing landscape, with shifting borders. A court ruling helps attorneys and consumers to understand what can be considered appropriate behavior regarding copyright protected materials.

Out-of-court settlements aren't necessarily inexpensive, however. A case against Los Angeles USD was settled out of court for $300,000 in fines plus attorney's fees (Business, 1999; Blair, 1998). In addition, the school was required to purchase at retail value all the computer software that had been installed illegally. The total cost for the incident amounted to about $5 million! So while an out-of-court settlement may reduce stress simply to have it behind, the option may not be a good one in terms of finances. A good attorney who specializes in intellectual property is the best person to consult in such a situation. She can analyze the situation and determine if the likelihood of winning a court case might make out of court settlement a poor idea.

WHY WORRY, WHY BOTHER?

Perhaps you have heard that schools are such "small potatoes" that big producers and publishers don't really care because a school doesn't have deep enough pockets for anyone to get a big settlement. You may have even heard that schools are exempt from copyright suits.

Don't believe it! Schools encounter copyright actions on a daily basis. Most are quickly resolved in a professional manner, and no public record exists. These types of actions are the type for which one can do no research. The author maintains a database of copyright infringement actions against schools at <www.carolsimpson.com>. There you can see a sampling of a variety of copyright actions told in the voices of those close to the situations.

Copyright compliance is as much an ethical issue as a legal one. Does one take something that belongs to another and appropriate it? Of course not! One would not walk into the crowded lunch line in the cafeteria and take a dessert without paying for it. "Taking something that doesn't belong to me?" the teacher declares indignantly. "I would never do such a thing, especially with students watching!" But the same person might stand in front of a class and instruct, "See how we can right click on this graphic and save it to our computers to use however we desire?" The law is a pain to keep up with, and there are few clear-cut rules, but the fact remains; the law is still the law, even if we don't like it. Those who don't like the law should work to change it, not just ignore it.

CHAPTER 2

Public Domain

A work not protected by copyright is considered to be in the public domain. Certain factors come into play when considering what is copyrightable:

- Only "creative" work can qualify for copyright protection. As we discussed in Chapter 1, facts are not eligible for the protection of copyright, but if someone were to write a narrative about certain facts, as long as there was a modicum of creativity involved, the expression of those facts would be protected by copyright.

- Only the author, or those to whom the author extended rights, can rightfully claim copyright.

- Works created by U.S. Federal government employees during the course of their duties–such as speeches of the U.S. President, acts of Congress, U.S. Government Web pages, etc.–are not eligible for copyright protection. However, as they may have used licensed art or other materials in their works, use caution. Keep in mind, too, that although federal government documents are in the public domain, not all governmental entities also place their materials in the public domain. Investigate this on a case-by-case, agency-by-agency basis. When in doubt, ask.

- Works, created during the period when a specific type of copyright notice was required, fell into the public domain if the notice was defective. For example, a copyright notice had to have the c-in-a-circle mark, or the word "copyright" to be considered valid. If your typewriter didn't have a copyright symbol and you typed a letter c between parentheses instead, your notice was considered to be defective and your copyright invalid. In such cases, the work immediately fell into the public domain if the work was published with the defective notice. Since 1989, however, copyright notice is no longer required.

- Works whose term of copyright has run the full course are no longer eligible for copyright protection. This class of works would include all those published before January 1, 1923.

- Works whose copyrights were not renewed, if they were covered during a period when copyright renewal was required, lost their copyright protection. Many silent films were not renewed after talking pictures became popular, so they are now in the public domain. Some other materials post-1923 are also now in the public domain as a result of nonrenewal.

- Some materials are dedicated to the public domain by their authors. The *Creative Commons* (<www.creativecommons.org>) has many examples of such works. Scholars contribute their works to this archive of public domain materials, in the hope that they will benefit scholarship and society as a whole.

Caveat: Just because a work has no notice of copyright does not mean that the work is in the public domain. Since 1989, the fact that a work has no copyright notice should not be taken to mean that the work is not protected by copyright.

How long does public domain last?

Since "public domain" means that a work is not covered by copyright, the rules regarding the length of copyright coverage do not apply. Currently, once a work has lost its copyright protection and has passed into the public domain, copyright protection cannot be regained on that work. Therefore, the public domain lasts, in effect, forever. There is an exception in Section 104 (a) that covers a particular class of unpublished works by foreign authors, but that exception will seldom apply in a K-12 school situation.

What can you do with Public Domain materials?

Public domain materials have no copyright restrictions. If a work is in the public domain, it may be reproduced, adapted, distributed, performed, displayed, and transmitted. However, it is essential to understand that only the **original** public domain work has these options. Subsequent modifications and adaptations may gain for their adaptors or creators a copyright on the additions or changes. For example, the original works of Beethoven are long in the public domain. However, no high school orchestras perform the **original** works of Beethoven because the originals are too difficult and require obsolete instruments; students perform copyrighted adaptations.

How do you find Public Domain materials?

Public domain materials are everywhere! There are even publishers who specialize in public domain materials. Educational publishers use many public domain materials because there are no costs to use them, and the publishers can edit the materials as they choose. English textbooks, for example, use materials by Shakespeare, Keats, and the like because they are free, as well as notable.

There are several sources to locate public domain materials. Not all the sources are free to use, though the public domain materials they help you locate are free to use, once you locate them in the original versions. Some of the best, such as *Public Domain Report* (<www.publicdomain.org>), are subscription Web sites. But they do offer samples of music, art, children's literature, drama, film, and literature. All have been scrupulously researched as to public domain status. The company has a public domain sheet music service, as well. Remember, you can arrange, translate, modify, and publish any of the public domain materials they provide, so the cost is negligible if you use the service to any degree. Most of the public domain Web sources offer a mix of copyright free and royalty free materials, so utilize them with caution.

What is the difference between "Copyright Free" and "Royalty Free?"

A work that is "copyright free" is in the public domain. There are no restrictions on its use. It may be copied, adapted, distributed, publicly performed or displayed and transmitted digitally if it is a sound recording. A work that is "royalty free" may still be protected by copyright (and usually is), but the copyright owner has elected to forgo collection of royalties for certain uses of the material.

HOW CAN I USE ROYALTY-FREE MATERIALS?

Royalty-free materials are usually governed by license. The license will explain in detail how the collection of materials can be used in your case. Typically, you can use the royalty-free art, or music, in standard broadcast situations or productions/publications without additional payment. The most usual prohibition on use of royalty-free material is to employ the items in another collection of similar items. For example, many collections of clip art are royalty free, but they are not copyright free. The artist or copyright owner does claim a copyright on the works, but the owner does not elect to charge a per use fee on the art as long as the person using the art abides by license restrictions. Upon reading the software license for the clip art, one discovers that use of the art in publication, Web pages, derivative works, etc. may be permitted, but it is expressly prohibited to use the work in another collection of clip art. Such a common prohibition might cause problems for teachers or librarians who are in the habit of collecting art from various free Web sites or clip art collections, and gathering them together by theme. By putting the royalty-free art into a clip art collection for her class, she has violated the license and the copyright of the art.

HAPTER 3

Fair Use

Copyright law provides several instances in which reproduction of copyrighted items is permissible. These exceptions to Section 106 (the section where the rights are defined) are considered the "fair use exemptions" and are found in Section 107 of the law.

It reads:

> Notwithstanding the provisions of sections 106 and 106A, the fair use of a copyrighted work, including such use by reproduction in copies or phonorecords or by any other means specified by that section, for purposes such as criticism, comment, news reporting, teaching (including multiple copies for classroom use), scholarship, or research, is not an infringement of copyright. In determining whether the use made of a work in any particular case is a fair use the factors to be considered shall include—
>
> 1. the purpose and character of the use, including whether such use is of a commercial nature, or is for nonprofit educational purposes;
>
> 2. the nature of the copyrighted work;
>
> 3. the amount and substantiality of the portion used in relation to the copyrighted work as a whole; and
>
> 4. the effect of the use upon the potential market for or value of the copyrighted work (U.S.C., Title 17, §107).

The Four Tests of Fair Use

©

1. The purpose and character of the use, including whether such use is of a commercial nature, or is for nonprofit educational purposes;

2. The nature of the copyrighted work;

3. The amount and substantiality of the portion used in relation to the copyrighted work as a whole; and

4. The effect of the use upon the potential market for or value of the copyrighted work (U.S.C., Title 17, §107).

These four factors are also known as the four tests of fair use. Basically what the law is saying is that Congress intends to protect the rights of the author while still allowing legitimate educational and research uses of copyrighted materials. Fair use is one of the most misunderstood aspects of copyright law. Common misconceptions about fair use include:

- Misconception #1–Schools can use any copyright protected materials they wish, because they are schools.

- Misconception #2–Using materials is okay if you don't make a profit.

- Misconception #3–Promoting someone's work by distributing copies is justification for free use.

- Misconception #4–Materials used "for the good of kids" absolves one of copyright liability.

WHAT IS IT?

Fair use provisions of the copyright law grant users conditional rights to use or reproduce certain copyrighted materials as long as the reproduction or use of those materials meets defined guidelines. As defined in the law, fair use balances the First Amendment free speech right with the rights of the author to control the use of his copyrighted work.

Fair use is not a right given to educators or any other person. Fair use is a defense applied in court to a charge of infringement. When a court considers a claim of fair use, it considers both the rights of the user and the rights of the author. The burden of proving fair use falls to the educator using the material, so thorough knowledge of copyright law and associated guidelines is essential for anyone using copyrighted works. As there is seldom a clear-cut fair use situation, it is incumbent upon the educator to know the conditions under which one may claim fair use.

DIFFERENCE BETWEEN FAIR USE AND GUIDELINES

Essentially there are two kinds of fair use:

1. Fair use as defined in the Copyright Act (statutory fair use). All people in the United States can avail themselves of this concept of fair use. The law defines the four factors that you must consider when making a claim of fair use, and the rights of both the creator and the person wishing to use the material are considered. More about these factors below.

2. Fair use is defined by several sets of guidelines designed for educators and librarians. These guidelines apply only to educational and library use of materials. Some guidelines are codified within the law itself (AV guidelines, TEACH Act) while others are agreed upon by outside organizations (multimedia guidelines).

For purposes of simplicity, guidelines are easier to learn and administer than going through the fair use tests, but if the guidelines don't permit a projected use, one may then apply the four tests of fair use to determine if the use might be fair.

Since educators have two forms of fair use available (statutory fair use and guidelines), assess a proposed use from both aspects to see if one will allow the use before abandoning the idea or attempting to license the use.

EXAMPLES OF FAIR USE ANALYSIS

Making a fair use assessment based on the factors outlined in the law (statutory fair use) is not a simple prospect. The law identifies four factors—some with sub-factors—that must be considered in any fair use assessment. While the law doesn't specify that any one of the factors has a greater weight than any of the others, in actual practice, courts have given more consideration to at least one of the four. We will discuss the four factors, then go through a sample analysis. Keep in mind that, in the absence of specific guidelines, all four tests of fair use will be considered in determining an appropriate application of the fair use doctrine.

Factor 1: Purpose and character of use

This first factor of fair use is probably the easiest one to assess. It is a two-part test. As with all the tests, apply this one objectively.

The first test of fair use encourages educational use of materials, but it has been interpreted to favor "transformative" uses (work that puts the borrowed material to a new or novel use), such as putting a quotation in a term paper. For example,

Figure 3.1: Balancing fair use factors

one court case stated that making low-resolution thumbnail-sized copies of images available elsewhere on the Internet was a "transformative" use (*Kelly v. Arriba Soft Corp.*, 280 F.3d 937 (9th Cir. 2002). Copying something without making changes generally is not transformative.

Part 1: Nonprofit educational use

Are you in a nonprofit public or private school, and is the use you are proposing for this entity? Such a use would get a favorable assessment on this portion of this factor, but even with a positive result here, one must continue to the other half of this factor plus the other three factors. For-profit schools, such as Edison Schools, some charter schools, and some private schools, would not receive a favorable assessment on this portion of Factor 1.

Part 2: Criticism, commentary, news reporting

Any of these choices can qualify a use on this half of the first factor. While intended to apply to the news industry, this selection could apply to the school newspaper, school television reports, etc.

Note that both halves of this factor do NOT need to be satisfied. For example, the local television station can still use a portion of a movie in a review under this factor (taking into account the rest of the factors, of course) even though it does not satisfy the first half of this factor regarding nonprofit educational setting. Transformation intensifies the effect of either of these sub parts, and may be becoming a third part in this area.

Factor 2: Nature of copyrighted work

Factor two of the four is also a two-pronged question. Neither half eliminates consideration as fair use, but having both on your side greatly enhances your fair use defense.

Part 1: Factual or creative?

Facts cannot receive copyright protection, but the expression of those facts can. For example, an encyclopedia article is written from and about factual material. The facts contained in the article are free to use, but the way the author of the encyclopedia article has expressed those facts is not. This is not always a black/white assessment. A painting of an historical event, for example, is both factual and creative.

Part 2: Published or not published?

The second half of this factor asks if the work is published. Unpublished works are more closely protected because the author/creator might not wish the material to be made public. Unpublished materials would be such things as letters, diaries, family photographs, emails, unpublished manuscripts, etc.

Factor 3: Amount of work used?

This factor asks "how much of the work will you use?" As a matter of practicality, the less you use, the better. If you want to use a short paragraph from a large Tom Clancy novel as an example of a metaphor, you are probably okay with that. However, if you want to use a haiku, you are going to be using **all** of it. Any time you use most or **all** of something, there will be questions about this factor.

Essence of the work

The term "essence of the work" is often tossed about when discussing how much one may use under Factor 3. This term is used to explain a short segment of a work that embodies the spirit of an entire work. If one uses something that embodies the entire piece within a small segment, one has–in essence–used the entire work.

This concept may be explained with an example. In the picture book, *Rosie's Walk* (Aladdin, 1971), the entire text of the book is spread across two pages at the beginning. The rest of the book consists only of pictures of Rosie the hen being pursued by a fox, blithely ignorant that she is on his dinner menu. So if one were to copy the two textual pages from this 32-page book, you would have copied a small portion of the book, yet you would have copied the text in its entirety!

Factor 4: Effect of use on market for or value of work

Courts historically have given this sole factor more importance than the other three in a fair use assessment. However, in the last five to ten years (since a court ruling said all factors must be equal), it has been reduced to a more equal (but not totally equal) weight. In essence, if your use would deprive someone of sales, this factor would come into play, and courts actually consider potential damage, rather than actual damages, when weighing this factor.

One must also consider that the "value of" fits in here. If your use would somehow disparage the original author, or his work, even in ways you might not imagine or agree with, this factor can become significant. Some people like to rationalize by saying that their use of a work actually promotes the original work. However, it is not up to the person borrowing the original work to make that decision. The copyright owner alone has the right to decide where and when his work will be publicized.

COMMERCIAL USE

Any commercial use of a work or portion of a work will yield a poor result on this factor (Crews, Message 23, Oct. 26, 1998). For schools, that would mean any use that transfers money, even if there is no net profit.

WHAT WOULD HAPPEN IF EVERYONE WERE TO ...

In analyzing a complex copyright situation, a copyright attorney once advised that the court, in assessing the final factor of fair use, must assess what would happen to the "market for or value of" the work if everyone were to do what you are proposing to do. In other words, the idea that you are just a small classroom in a rural school in middle America isn't the issue. The issue is that if everybody were to repeat this same behavior, what effect would that have on the market value of the work? For example, if every teacher made copies of an entire picture book for her class, you can easily see how the broad reproduction might affect the market for the book.

For example, if you sell year-books, and you have used unlicensed/nonpermissioned copyrighted graphics in the yearbook, this use would be considered "commercial." The same would hold true if you are selling CDs of the band concert, or t-shirts with a cartoon on them, or any other transaction involving copyright-protected materials used without license or permission.

VARIOUS TYPES OF GUIDELINES

In addition to the statutory fair use tests, various sets of guidelines have developed over the years. Since the original text of the law was too vague to be of much help in deciding if a particular use was permitted, the U.S. House of Representatives and the Senate held hearings in an effort to determine an equitable balance between the rights of copyright owners and those of the general public.

The hearings resulted in a set of guidelines, often referred to as the "Congressional Guidelines" or the "fair use guidelines." (See <www.lib.jmu.edu/org/mla/> and click on "Guidelines" in the left menu.) These guidelines are not law, but are interpreted to be the Congress' intent in enacting the law. The courts have taken this statement of intent into account when deciding cases of copyright infringement.

In addition to the Congressional guidelines that dealt with primarily print, there are also guidelines that have emerged from the wording in the law describing fair use of audiovisual and digital materials. Regulations on interlibrary loans and resource sharing, components of an active library program, followed. As technology advanced, presentation packages such as PowerPoint stretched the limits of fair use. Pressure from educators on producers finally yielded a set of industry guidelines to govern the use of copyright-protected materials in these types of presentations.

The Digital Millennium Copyright Act established some guidelines for schools that put materials on the Web, through the creation of a copyright agent program. Each "online service provider" (most schools qualify as an OSP) can protect itself against copyright actions by establishing a position called "the agent." The agent follows certain procedures to monitor copyright claims for the site, and the sponsoring organization is rewarded with limited immunity from prosecution.

Guidelines took a giant leap forward with the passage of the TEACH Act, codifying guidelines for using copyrighted materials in distance learning situations. New advances in course distribution required a parallel reorganization of fair use permissions to enable online classes to have similar fair use of materials that face-to-face classes had enjoyed for many years.

Each time technology took a leap forward, fair use guidelines followed behind, trying to keep up. Unfortunately, when guidelines were created to handle the newer technologies, older guidelines were not updated to match. Hence, you will find that what is okay in one medium is not okay in another.

GENERAL PUBLIC VS. SCHOOLS

Sometimes the restrictions of guidelines will not allow enough of some medium to meet the teaching need of a student or teacher. For example, the multimedia guidelines allow using up to 30 seconds or 10 percent of a song in a multimedia presentation, whichever is less. For a typical rock song, 10 percent is 18 seconds, so the limit is the lower of 18 and 30. However, suppose that a musical phrase that the teacher wants to use is 20 seconds in length. Does that mean the segment is out because it exceeds the 18 second limitation? Or does it mean that the teacher must truncate the phrase to be able to use it? Not necessarily. The teacher can go through the four-test analysis that is available to all citizens. If the use can pass the four tests, she can use the 20 seconds with confidence.

SCHOOLS VS. LIBRARIES

As pointed out earlier, everyone has certain fair use rights. Schools get a special set of fair use rights to help them educate students. Libraries get another set of special guidelines to help them achieve their civic mission. School libraries get the best of all possible worlds, since they can claim the school exemptions, the library exemptions, and the fair use exemptions afforded all citizens. The school library exemptions don't extend to the parent school, however. Only activities within the library are acceptable candidates for the library exemptions.

The best part of having the library exemptions may be that if you have a library you probably have a librarian. School librarians are the only educators who routinely receive an education on copyright law during their training. The librarian is a resource person who can help students, faculty, and administrators puzzle out the conundrum that is copyright. Look upon your librarian as the copyright consultant, not the copyright cop.

CHAPTER 4

Print Materials in Schools

B ecause the four factors cited in Section 107 were less than clear, representatives of affected education and publishing groups met to work out much more
specific explanations of the law. The result was endorsed by Congress when it was
read into the Congressional Record. These Congressional Guidelines (1976)
<http://www.lib.jmu.edu/org/mla/Guidelines/Accepted%20Guidelines/
Educational%20Photocopying.aspx>, as they are called, are not law, *per se*, but they
were written to indicate legislative intent and are used as benchmarks against which
copyright infringement is gauged.

These guidelines were developed primarily for print materials, because print
material was predominant in 1976 when the guidelines were written. While there are
specific limits and restrictions based on the format of material, there are also some
general tests imposed on all educational uses of copyrighted works. These tests are
more concrete and easier to apply to educational and library copying than are the fair
use factors. The additional tests are those of brevity (defined by specific lengths and
numbers of items), spontaneity (see following questions), and cumulative effect.

There should be an affirmative answer to both of the following questions before a claim of fair use may be made under these guidelines:

1. Copying is at the instance and inspiration of the individual teacher, and

2. The inspiration and decision to use the work and the moment of its use for maximum teaching effectiveness are so close in time that it would be unreasonable to expect a timely reply to a request for permission.

Essentially these spontaneity questions restrict educators from having materials (or television programs) copied in anticipation of demand. All requests for duplication, whether photocopies or off-air taping, must happen so close to the time the teacher will use the materials that the teacher doesn't have enough time to request and receive permission. In other words, an administrator, department head, librarian, or other person in a position of authority may not direct teachers or librarians to copy materials under the fair use exemption. In addition, a teacher's superior may not dictate to the teacher that copyright-protected materials must be copied. A supervisor may *suggest* specific materials, but it is the responsibility of the individual teacher to decide to make the copies. This requirement is often called a "bottom up" copying scheme as opposed to a "top down" order.

What typical activities are covered?

The photocopy machine is probably the biggest danger spot in the school from the standpoint of print copying. Teachers photocopy materials at an astounding rate, and they do not always have the authority to make multiple copies of the items they are copying. While the print guidelines are very specific about how much and how many times something may be copied, and also specify items which may *never* be copied, few teachers or administrators have ever seen the guidelines.

The following is not a complete list of the types of print copying activities that are possible or even common in schools. But knowing the rules for these activities will provide guidance to other types of activities. **Remember, if you have permission you can do whatever the permission allows, regardless of what the law says.**

Photocopying–issues

Typical photocopying issues to which schools will want to pay particular attention include:

- Photocopying any consumable materials such as workbooks (whether or not the book is still in print or in adoption) absent permission of the copyright owner.

- Photocopying more materials per term or year (depending on the length of the course) than allowed in the guidelines.

- Using photocopies to substitute for purchase of materials (as in making copies of textbook chapters rather than buying a copy of the text when you are a few short).

- Administrators or curriculum coordinators directing teachers or entire grade levels or courses to photocopy protected materials. Such decisions may only be made by the teachers themselves, individually, within the frequency limits.

- Not getting permission to repeatedly copy materials after the first fair use.

- Copying student work to retain as exemplars.

Phonorecords–issues

No, we aren't talking about 12-inch black vinyl discs. An audio-recording of a print work is called a "phonorecord." It is important to note that reading a book onto a cassette tape or MP3 player is exactly the same thing, according to the law, as putting that book on the photocopier and copying every page.

Graphics–issues

While the guidelines do address graphics for instruction, many of the graphics used in schools are used for decoration, not for instruction. The types of graphics issues that schools will need to pay particular attention to include:

- Copying/enlarging cartoon characters, greeting card graphics, images from books/coloring books for the purpose of decoration.

- Using graphic characters on school t-shirts, book bags, signs, etc.

- Using characters from library books to create murals, or other decorative elements.

Murals–issues

Schools need to be concerned when the mural artist uses the work of others in the mural. The work of others can be famous paintings (painted after 1923 and not in the public domain) or uses–more commonly–famous book characters such as the Cat in the Hat, or Disney characters. These instantly recognizable characters are not only protected by copyright but they are also protected by trademark in most cases.

Scanning–issues

Changing format on the scan is the biggest problem you will encounter with this method of reproduction. When one creates a scan, not only do you create a copy but you create a *digital* copy of an analog work. Digital copies may be copied infinitely without any of the degradation that is common to analog copies such as photocopies. Producers are exceptionally nervous about allowing their material to be digitized, fearing that it will "escape" and be lost forever.

What rights are affected?

Of the reserved rights of the copyright holder, several are of particular import in issues of print reproduction. Those rights include:

- **Reproduction:** Making copies is how a print copyright owner makes money. If you make the copies locally, the copyright owner gets no money from your copies.

- **Distribution:** Copyright owners get to decide where (or if) their works will be distributed.

- **Adaptation:** When you make changes in print materials, you are adapting them. Perhaps you want to translate a work into Spanish for your Hispanic students. This typical activity is considered adaptation and is within the rights of the copyright owner.

- **Display:** Print materials are displayed when they are put in a public place. Display could include book covers on bulletin boards; posting student work in the halls, or on a Web page; newsletters and yearbooks.

These rights may be modified by specific educational or fair use exemptions or other doctrines such as first sale.

WHAT GUIDELINES AFFECT PRINT MATERIALS?

When considering what fair uses one may make of print materials, there are several things to keep in mind. First, is the material protected at all? Remember that anything published before 1923 is in the public domain in the United States. Materials published after 1923 but before 1978 that were not registered appropriately, or renewed, are also in the public domain. You may use public domain materials for any purpose whatsoever.

If you find that the material is, indeed, protected, you may decide to seek a fair use defense to your use of the materials. You have two choices: find a set of guidelines that apply to the materials you wish to use, or apply the statutory four tests of fair use. Finding that the materials are print, you may elect to use the print guidelines to see if your proposed use is within the limits of the guidelines. If your use exceeds the guidelines, you may go through a fair use analysis to determine if your use may be considered fair via that route.

When the 1976 law was passed, there were no guidelines. There was only the fair use section of the law (section 107). The law is cryptic and difficult for laypeople to understand. Representative Robert Kastenmeier of the House Judiciary Subcommittee headed a House committee that worked with publishers and education representatives to clarify the fair use definitions codified in the law, and to give educators understandable, workable limits for fair use. These limits are known collectively as the Kastenmeier Report, the classroom photocopying guidelines, or sometimes the print guidelines.

Kastenmeier report

The first half of the report covers print works (specifically books and periodicals) and the second half includes guidelines on the use of printed music. Also appended are short guidelines on replacement copying and repair of damaged materials (Special Interest Video Sales Group, 1995).

SINGLE COPIES FOR TEACHERS

A teacher may copy (or ask to have copied) for the purposes of research, teaching, or preparation for teaching any of the following:

- A single copy of a chapter from a book.

- A single copy of an article from a periodical or newspaper.

- A single copy of a short story, short essay, or short poem, even if it is contained in a collection.

- A single copy of a chart, graph, diagram, drawing, cartoon, or picture from a book, periodical, or newspaper.

The teacher may retain the single copies of these materials in files for personal or research use or for use in teaching. The Congressional guidelines provide some limitations on these options. There are four significant prohibitions to the print permission, three of which have application to single copies for teachers:

- Copying shall not be used to create or to replace or substitute for anthologies, compilations, or collective works. In other words, you can't create your own books by gathering bits and pieces from other sources. This would include notebooks of editorial cartoons, comic strips, series of essays, and the like.

- There shall be no copying from works intended to be "consumable" in the course of study or of teaching. These include workbooks, exercises, standardized tests and test booklets, and answer sheets, and like consumable material.

- Copying shall not substitute for the purchase of books, publishers' reprints or periodicals; be directed by higher authority; or be repeated with respect to the same item by the same teacher from term to term.

The prohibitions are significant because they deal with guidelines often breached in daily school and library practice. A teacher may find some particular item that seems relevant to a course. While copying some portion of the text is acceptable, copying more than the limited chapter, article, essay, or chart described in the law previously discussed would be considered substituting for the personal purchase of the work and would therefore be in violation of the Congressional guidelines and of the copyright law itself. Sometimes a work may be out of print, and a teacher will attempt to justify copying the entire work because it is not available in the marketplace. However, out of print is not the same as out of copyright. By making unauthorized copies beyond the chapter/essay/article limit, the teacher bypasses the permissions and royalty to which the copyright owner would be entitled.

Similarly, since copying may not be "directed by higher authority," an administrator, curriculum director, supervisor, or department head cannot direct a teacher or other staff member to copy copyrighted materials under fair use for whatever purpose. An individual teacher must initiate the copying for that teacher's use. An example of violation of this aspect of the guidelines would be a principal telling a teacher to copy a specific article on an aspect of classroom management. The principal may ask the teacher to *read* the article but cannot order the teacher to *copy* the article. The teacher may, however, decide to copy the article for files or for reading at a more convenient time. This decision originated with the teacher; hence, there is no violation.

MULTIPLE COPIES FOR CLASSROOM USE

Copying in multiple units for student use in a classroom setting is completely permissible if certain tests are met. An instructor may not make more than one copy of the item for each student in the course, and each item copied must be used for classroom use or for discussion. Additionally, each copy must include a notice of copyright.

The requirement of notice of copyright is the most often neglected aspect of this section of the guidelines. Each copy must have a notice of the copyright holder. Ordinarily this can be as simple as a notation on the margin of the page such as "Copyright 2001, Big Publishing Co." Failure to include this notice is a violation of the Digital Millennium Copyright Act because it removes what is known as *copyright management information*.

The three tests that each instance of copying must meet are brevity, spontaneity, and cumulative effect. These tests are very specific in nature, and each copy must meet all the criteria for each test.

BREVITY

Poetry: If a poem is less than 250 words and is printed on not more than two pages, it may be copied in its entirety. If the poem is longer than 250 words, only 250 words may be copied. The law does allow an unfinished line to be included if the 250-word limit should happen to fall in the middle of a line.

Prose: If a complete article, story, or essay is less than 2,500 words, it may be copied in its entirety. For other types of prose, such as a play, a novel, or a letter, a copy must not be more than 1,000 words or 10 percent of the whole, whichever is less. No matter how short the work, one may legitimately copy an excerpt of 500 words. In other words, if a work is only 1,000 words in total, a teacher may copy 500 words even though that amount exceeds the 10 percent guideline.

Exception: Only two pages of a picture book may be copied as long as those two pages do not comprise more than 10 percent of the text of the book. Graphic novels were not invented when these guidelines were written, but one could make a good case that they would fall into a similar exception.

Illustration: One chart, graph, drawing, cartoon, diagram, or picture may be copied per book or periodical issue. These copies must be photocopies or other exact copies. Modifying the illustration in any way violates the author's right of adaptation.

SPONTANEITY

The rationale for the spontaneity rule is that the idea and decision to use the work and the moment it will be used for maximum teaching effectiveness are so close in time that it would be unreasonable to expect a timely reply to a request for permission. "Unreasonable" and "timely" are subject to some degree of latitude. As a rule of thumb, allow about three weeks for a reply. If teachers know at least three weeks ahead of time that they will need to copy something for use in class, they should write for permission. If they do not receive a reply in time, they could then proceed with the copying since there is not sufficient time to send a second query. Any copying beyond the first time would require permission.

CUMULATIVE EFFECT

The cumulative effect guidelines want to assure that copying is not substituting for purchase of books and periodicals. To comply with this test, the copying must be done for only one course. For example, a teacher may make copies of a poem for all freshman English classes (one copy per student), but may not copy the same poem for her sophomore English classes.

The guidelines limit the number of copies that may be made from a single source or author during a school year (or a semester or quarter if this isn't a full-year class). These limitations include:

- A teacher may make class copies of one short poem, article, story, or essay or two excerpts from the same author during one term (year or semester or quarter).

If the copies are taken from a collective work (a book of poetry or essays by multiple authors, for example), the teacher is limited to three or fewer items during a class term.

- Periodical articles are also limited to three or fewer items copied from one periodical volume (not issue) during one term.

- Current news articles from newspapers and magazines are exempt from this requirement. When an item ceases to become "current news" is not defined, but a two-month window would be generous.

- No more than nine instances of such multiple copying can occur for one course during one class term.

While the above rules are very specific, you must also consider the four **prohibitions** to the print permission when determining fair use.

COPIES FOR DISABLED STUDENTS

A modification to the rule against copying and adaptation permits institutions serving the blind and physically handicapped to acquire or make adaptive copies in Braille or other formats (17 U.S.C. § 121). There are specific regulations about the format of the copies and who may use them. These rules cover students who are unable to use standard print works because of visual deficiencies, or because they are physically handicapped and cannot hold a book or turn its pages. It does *not* address the needs of the dyslexic or slow learner. Those students who qualify under this law must be identified through the Library of Congress Division of Blind and Physically Handicapped, or through one of the state library branches. Application requires certification of the disability by medical personnel. The "other formats" includes reading books onto cassette tapes, for example, but one must pay particular attention to the format of tape specified in the law.

As of December 3, 2004, a new amendment to copyright law came via the Individuals with Disabilities Education Improvement Act of 2004. The new requirements allow certain technologies to be employed to assist "print disabled" (which would include diagnosed dyslexic) students. These materials will be able to be produced locally only if such materials are not available for purchase.

The law also provided for the establishment of the National Instructional Materials Access Center under the auspices of the American Printing House for the Blind. The law directs a new National Instructional Materials Accessibility Standard that will be available solely for the conversion of print materials into accessible formats for print-disabled students. However, the new standard and exemptions only apply to required textbooks. Library materials and supplementary materials are not addressed in the new law. Authorization for services under this law will require certification through the State Library or the Library of Congress Division of Blind and Physically Handicapped. Both require certification by a medical professional that the individual is unable to use standard print materials. (Individuals, 2005).

PRINT PERMISSION ISSUES

If a teacher knows that a particular item will be used year to year or term to term, the safest course is to write for permission. However, if the teacher requests permission but gets no response by the time the material is needed, the teacher may make the needed copies–once. If the teacher hasn't gotten permission to make copies by the second time the materials are needed, she needs to locate something else to use. Always remember: The publisher or copyright owner is not required to reply to your request. If you get no reply, you should assume the answer is "no."

CONSUMABLE MATERIALS

Consumable materials include workbooks, tests, standardized tests, answer sheets, and worksheets among other forms of consumables such as cut-outs, templates, and patterns intended to be destroyed in making the item. The prohibitions on multiple copying state that "there shall be no copying of or from materials intended to be consumable." Pattern books, such as knitting books or woodworking plans, probably don't qualify as consumable and would likely be afforded the protection of other printed works, but dress patterns printed on tissue are likely intended to be destroyed to an extent in making the item.

PERIODICALS

Those guidelines affecting the copying of periodical materials are:

- The copying must be done for only one course.
- Only one entire article or two excerpts may be copied from the same author.
- No more than three items from the same periodical volume may be copied during one class term (year or semester, depending on the course).
- No more than nine items (of which periodicals may be some or all) may be copied in multiples per course during one class term.

Documents in the public domain, such as periodicals or monographs from the Department of Education or ERIC, do not count in the total copies per year as there is no restriction on duplication of public domain materials. Any materials for which you have explicit permission to copy in multiple also do not count in the total.

The general prohibitions on multiple copying apply to periodicals, also. Those prohibitions specify that copies may not be used to create or substitute for anthologies or compilations. The prohibitions state that the copies do not have to be "accumulated" to fall under this rule. "Accumulated" in this case means collecting the copies and distributing them all at the same time, as if they were together in a booklet. The articles may be copied and used separately and still violate this prohibition.

Additionally, copying must not substitute for the purchase of a subscription to the periodical or publisher's reprints; it must not be ordered by a higher authority (such as a lead teacher, administrator, or curriculum supervisor) and the same items may not be copied in succeeding class terms. Of course, the student may not be charged for the copies beyond the actual cost of the copies. The most significant consideration in this list is that of financial impact on the copyright owner. If the proposed fair use copying were to be repeated widely by many others, would such copying have an adverse effect on the copyright holder's revenues? If so, the use is undoubtedly not fair for this factor.

The lone exception to the rules on copying from periodicals is that of articles from current news periodicals (e.g. *Time*, *Newsweek*) and newspapers and the current news sections of other periodicals. Using the Guidelines for guidance, copying such articles is in compliance. The only question would be how "current" the article is. While no guidelines exist to specify the amount of time allotted to "currency," a window of several weeks would not be inappropriate and would certainly be justifiable, especially around vacation periods where an article might be published but the class does not meet for a two-week span of time.

GRAPHICS

Making a single copy of a graph or illustration from a book is acceptable if the copy is for personal research or study, and multiple copies of a single graphic are authorized for a class under the standard print fair use guidelines:

- Copying must be at the instance and inspiration of the teacher and so close in time to the required use that receipt of permission would be impossible;
- The copy is for only one course in the school;
- There are not more than nine occurrences of multiple copying for that course; and
- Not more than one graphic is copied per book or periodical.

Adaptation is a bigger dilemma. By taking an artist's work and enlarging, modifying, or converting it to another medium, a teacher usurps the creator's (or more accurately, the copyright holder's) right to determine how the image will be used.

SCANNERS

The scanner has jolted the world of print copyright. Virtually any image can now be transformed into bits and bytes for incorporation into graphics packages, desktop publishing documents, and multimedia presentations. As stated previously, the original copyright holder retains the rights of reproduction, adaptation, and display, among others. Scanning a copyrighted illustration may be a copyright violation of any of those three rights. A student may use a scanned copyrighted image in a report, but the student must retain ownership of the report once it is graded. The teacher may not retain that report (or a copy of it), nor may she reproduce it for a workshop. If the work is a multimedia presentation, it may only be displayed for the students and teachers in the class for which it was prepared (see the section on Multimedia for more details).

CHAPTER 5

Audiovisual Materials in Schools

he law defines audiovisual as follows:

"Audiovisual works" are works that consist of a series of related images which are intrinsically intended to be shown by the use of machines, or devices such as projectors, viewers, or electronic equipment, together with accompanying sounds, if any, regardless of the nature of the material objects, such as films or tapes, in which the works are embodied. 17 U.S.C. § 101

Section 110 of the Copyright Act of 1976 was written, in part, to address the needs of producers of audiovisual materials who were concerned that their property was not being adequately protected under the old law. The new law clarified many ambiguities, though often not in favor of educators.

> *The same fair use guidelines that apply to print materials do not apply to audiovisuals. There are differing guidelines for print, audiovisuals, multimedia, and distance learning, and the guidelines are not at all consistent.*

Because of the nature of the audiovisual medium, producers worry not only about unauthorized copies but also about losing profits from unauthorized performances of the protected works. Producers of music recordings, movies, and television programs make their money from licensing those works for public exhibition and broadcast as well as from direct sales, so they are especially wary about what end users will do with the copy they have purchased. Had Congress allowed as free a rein for copying audiovisuals as they permitted for print materials, these media producers feared they would be cheated of profits that were rightfully theirs.

The key to understanding the audiovisual guidelines is recognizing that Congress, when writing the law, wished to provide support to teachers in a classroom while presenting content to students. Beyond that, they had little sympathy for a school's request to be exempt from the requirements of copyright. As long as direct teaching is involved, teachers are fairly free to use video and its cousins within the classroom. The primary problems administrators have with the guidelines are that teachers know there is more to school than just class, and there is more to learning than the set curriculum. Enrichment, reward, and relaxation are all valid parts of the educational experience, but they are not ones that Congress elected to support through exemption from the requirements of copyright law. Once that basic concept is internalized, the audiovisual exemptions fall into place.

What typical activities are covered?

It is very important to remember that this section of the law covers video, film-strips, sound recordings, graphics, and all other nonprint formats that are not multimedia or distance learning.

Because school is a public place (in other words, it is not a private home), *any* performance of a copyrighted work in a school is considered a public performance. Public performance is a right reserved to the copyright holder. Certain types of public performances, however, are permitted under the exemptions for audiovisual performances included in section 110(1). If a particular showing should happen not to meet the requirements for exemption, does that mean the audiovisual work cannot be shown? Not at all. It just means that the showing isn't exempt from the requirements of public performance. Public performance of audiovisual media without an exemption requires one of three things:

1. Permission from the copyright owner to hold a public performance.

2. A license from a rights broker that covers the work to be shown.

3. Payment of royalties to the copyright owner or his agent.

Movies–issues

The primary issue involved with showing films is non-instructional showings or peri-instructional showings. A secondary issue involves archival copies. The key thing to keep in mind as you go through the explanations and rationale for the audiovisual rules is that the members of Congress who passed these rules must report to both educators and publishers/producers. Alas, because educators consume resources and publishers/producers create them and pay taxes on the income derived from them, Congress leaned toward the side of producers in this aspect of fair use.

TV/cable/satellite–issues

The issues surrounding television and cable programming are similar to those involving film and video. Non-curricular and peri-curricular showings are common, though non-permitted. Because many of the useful curricular-related programs show at night and on weekends, teachers would like to tape programs for showing at a better time of day, or a better time of the school year (when they are studying the topic of the program). Recording programs and retaining them is a different issue than just showing the program, as in the case of video. With off-air recording, you are actually making a copy of the program as well as performing it.

Occasionally the local cable company will provide a feed of the basic cable lineup, and showing those programs live is perfectly okay if your school is a subscriber. However, subscribing at home allows you to tape and retain programs for use at your convenience, but use at school (of programs taped at home or at school) is for public performance and therefore does not enjoy the same permissions as recording for private use at home. See more about taping from cable/satellite in the section on off-air taping.

Web–issues

Until the TEACH Act was enacted, "transmissions" of audiovisual works were prohibited. Now, under the requirements of TEACH, some transmissions of audiovisual materials are allowed. See the chapters on the Internet and distance learning for complete details.

Sound recordings–issues

Sound recordings include both music and spoken word recordings. The recordings may be on any type of medium, from wire recordings to vinyl to digital recordings. While digital recordings have amazing clarity and depth of sound, a person can copy a digital sound recording with perfect reproduction an infinite number of times. The recording industry felt the effects of this simple technique as far back as 2002, citing significant drops in sales and profits. (RIAA, 2002).

What rights are affected?

Producers of audiovisual materials are anxious about their materials. They apply various technical protection measures to prevent copying or illegal performance of their works. Their reasons include potential violation of the following rights:

- **Reproduction**: Copies, especially digital copies, mean unlimited reproduction at perfect quality. With the history of the decline of the recording industry after MP3 filesharing, producers are understandably nervous about allowing copies for any reason.

- **Distribution**: Distribution of copies is the copyright owner's biggest worry. The copies made could be distributed via networks like MP3 files or on disc. Distribution of television programs and video can occur when using a video distribution system, or through cable networks or microwave transmission.

- **Adaptation**: Any time you change the format of a work, you have created an adaptation. Changing a work from VHS to DVD or streaming video is an adaptation. So is taking clips and making a separate tape of excerpts (equivalent to an anthology of print works). If you expurgate a work (remove offensive words or scenes) you have also created an adaptation.

- **Public performance**: Any performance that happens in a school is a public performance. "Public" is defined as follows:

  . . .a place open to the public or at any place where a substantial number of persons outside of a normal circle of a family and its social acquaintances is gathered. . .

  Any display or performance of a copyrighted work under these circumstances would require a license. The gray area of this definition is the "substantial number." Putting motion media onto the open Web can certainly be considered a public performance since you have made it accessible to the world via the web.

- **Public display**: Section 101 of 17 U.S.C. defines a display: To "display" a work means to show a copy of it, either directly or by means of a film, slide, television image, or any other device or process or, in the case of a motion picture or other audiovisual work, to show individual images nonsequentially. (17 U.S.C. § 101). Where a display becomes "public" has always been an issue of concern. Obviously, the same definition of public applies here as it does for public performance. Remember, however, that there will be some fair use and guideline exemptions that will come into play.

- **Digital transmission**: Digital transmission was added to the rights of the copyright holder with the passage of the Digital Millennium Copyright Act. Digital transmission had been a concern of music producers once they realized that Internet radio was streaming perfect digital copies of their songs to anyone who cared to save the files on their local computer systems. Since (with tongue firmly in cheek) a CD only has perhaps one good cut, why pay for an entire CD when you can grab the "good one" for no cost via Internet radio? As a result of this concern, significant royalties must be collected for each listener of a recording digitally transmitted. The DMCA did not provide for any specific educational exemptions for digital transmission, but the various media would still fall under the existing TEACH Act if they met the requirements.

What guidelines affect AV materials?

Rules for using audiovisual materials are included in section 110(1) of 17 U.S.C., the current copyright law, so this will be a question of law, not one of externally developed guidelines. The actual wording says:

> Notwithstanding the provisions of section 106, the following are not infringements of copyright:
>
> (1) performance or display of a work by instructors or pupils in the course of face-to-face teaching activities of a nonprofit educational institution, in a classroom or similar place devoted to instruction, unless, in the case of a motion picture or other audiovisual work, the performance, or the display of individual images, is given by means of a copy that was not lawfully made under this title, and that the person responsible for the performance knew or had reason to believe was not lawfully made;

The rules are written in legalese, not in eduspeak, so it may take a bit of translation to explain the significance of the five factors included.

 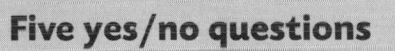
Five yes/no questions

Explaining audiovisual fair use can be condensed into five yes/no questions, based on the factors set forth in the law. **Any** answer of **no** on the following questions means that **public performance rights** are required to show the film in that circumstance.

1 Are you a nonprofit educational institution?

The use here must truly be nonprofit. Interestingly, you don't have to make a profit to be "for profit." You only have to try to make a profit. An Edison school or a for-profit day care center would have a **no** here.

2. Will you show the video in a classroom or similar place?

A "similar place" could be the auditorium, gymnasium, cafeteria, multipurpose room, library, theatre, band hall, natatorium, field house, etc. A "similar place" probably would not be the local pizza parlor (unless this were a business class and they were watching a film on restaurant management) or on a bus on the way to a band competition.

3. Will the video be used with instructors and pupils in the course of face-to-face teaching activities in a regularly scheduled class?

This factor means that the use is for direct teaching in class. Reward, enrichment, and supplemental activities are not qualifying activities. Extracurricular and babysitting activities are also not covered here.

4. Are you showing a legally acquired copy?

There are many ways to legally acquire a copy of an audiovisual work. As long as someone has legitimately paid for the copy, you are probably clear on this factor.

Ways you can get a "legally acquired" copy include:

   a. *Library:* You may use a copy of an audiovisual work owned by your school library.

b. *Student or teacher*: You may legally use a copy of a work owned by a teacher, a student, or a student's parents, as long as the work isn't taped from cable or off-air beyond the taping guidelines (see off-air taping section).

c. *Borrowed from library*: You may use a copy borrowed from the public library, a university or community college library, or from a regional media library.

d. *Rented from video store*: A copy rented from your local video store may be used as long as the teacher can answer **yes** to all five of the AV exemption questions.

e. *Taped programs*: A video taped off an over air channel (or with permission of the copyright holder from a cable/satellite channel) is an acceptable source to answer **yes** to this question. (See off-air taping guidelines section).

While you needn't demand receipts from students and teachers, a cautious approach would dictate that outside videos be accompanied by a statement from the owner verifying ownership. Should the copy later be determined to be fraudulent, the school administrator then has a solid case she had no knowledge that the tape was in violation.

5. Face-to-face teaching activities

This factor of AV fair use is generally the most difficult to meet because this is where Congress states that they expect to see the direct teach piece in the analysis. In other words, the display of the work must be related to the lesson at hand, not simply related to some type of lesson past or a lesson to come. For example, the freshman English curriculum might require the students to read Shakespeare's *Romeo and Juliet* in September each year. However, the English teacher needs some time to prepare final exams later in the semester, so she decides to show the Franco Zefferelli film of the play to occupy her students while she works on the exam months after the class has studied the play. Such use of the video would probably not be within the fair use exemption since the class is no longer studying the play. A good rule of thumb to determine if use of a video is acceptable is to ask, Is this an integral part of the unit I am teaching right now? If the answer is **no**, then the showing is probably a public performance.

Additionally, beware of what might be called "general cultural value." Certainly there are many wonderfully educational videos on the market and perhaps in your library or personal video collection. However, showing these types of videos to a class without a specific curricular objective is not permitted under the "face-to-face" rule. If the objective isn't specified in the curriculum guide for this particular class, showing a video on that topic is a public performance and license or permission is required. Keep in mind that what is "curricular" for one class might not be part of the curriculum for another, no matter how "educational" the topic might be.

Umbrella licenses

Unless there is a specific teaching goal documented in a district curriculum guide or state standard, one may reliably count on the need for a performance license. Several vendors sell "umbrella licenses" that permit the school or library to show non-curricular films and videos from limited lists of producers. There are pros and cons to these licenses. A library-only license makes the librarian (and the library) the local "babysitter." Whenever the PE teacher is out, the kids are sent to the library to see movies to keep them entertained. If you have a building-wide license, teachers become lax in their use of video. The primary vendor of these licenses is Movie Licensing USA <www.movlic.com>.

Home use only

Many videos have a "home use only" notice. Some libraries and schools are fearful that using tapes so labeled will place them in jeopardy. The truth is that simply placing a "home use only" notice on a video does not restrict a school from lending a copy owned by the library or using the program if the use otherwise meets all of the fair use criteria set forth above.

Once a tape has been sold, the "right of first sale" states that copyright owner's exclusive distribution right to that copy has ceased (Reed, 1989, p. 2). The transfer of the right of distribution is the essential transaction that allows libraries to lend books and other materials. Note that only the right of distribution has ceased. The right of performance and display still resides with the copyright owner.

> **Caution:** Watch carefully for producers or suppliers who sell you a license to a program rather than the program itself. Licensing a program is a way for a copyright owner to retain the distribution right since there is no actual sale. If you purchase a license to a program, you will be subject to any restrictions the copyright owner may choose to impose, including restricting your right to lend the program.

Some practices that are never acceptable with film or video include:

- Making an anthology or collection from clips or excerpts.
- Transferring the work to another medium, e.g., film to video, or video to computer disk **unless** the medium on which the work is stored is obsolete based on the legal definition of "obsolete" **and** the work is not available for purchase in a newer medium (with a small exception for some distance learning uses under the TEACH act).
- Using a program for recreation or reward without acquiring performance rights.

Off-air taping guidelines

A lot of misinformation floats around about what may be taped and what may be retained. The number one consideration to keep in mind when trying to determine a tape's status is "who taped this and when?" Many court cases have determined that a private individual may tape–for the purposes of "time shifting"–anything broadcast over the public airwaves or from cable channels to which the individual subscribes. The person may then retain the tapes without penalty. But the tape is only for the use of that individual, his or her immediate family, and their circle of friends.

The key to knowing what you may and may not tape is knowing how the program is getting to the television set. For school use, programs may be freely recorded from regular broadcast channels. Broadcast channels are those VHF and UHF channels one can ordinarily receive via a regular television antenna. If a particular channel is simultaneously rebroadcast on cable, the actual recording may be made from the cable transmission. This can be an advantage in instances when the cable signal is better than the broadcast signal, or when the recorder is already hooked up to the cable instead of an antenna.

"Air" vs. cable vs. satellite

But what about all those wonderful cable channels like Disney or Nickelodeon or Discovery or The History Channel? There are no fair use rights for exclusively cable channels. Decisions to tape a particular program must be researched on the basis of granted rights. Since reproduction rights reside with the copyright holder, the ability of a school to tape a program and retain it for any amount of time is wholly at the whim of the copyright holder. Many of these channels offer educators' guides that enumerate the available rights on a program-by-program basis. The Cable in the Classroom Web site <www.ciconline.org> also offers retention rights information and addresses of producers so that permissions and supplemental materials may be requested.

Satellite programming will have the same restrictions as cable broadcasts. Programs broadcast by satellite may not be taped for school use without specific permission of the copyright holder. Deliberately de-scrambling encrypted satellite signals is a federal offense.

A librarian cannot tape a program just because she knows someone will ask for it after the fact. If the librarian has recorded the program at the specific request of a teacher, she may fulfill the appeal; otherwise, she will have to disappoint.

Copies taped off-air must include all copyright information, usually found in the credits at the end of the program. The program need not be shown in its entirety, but the program itself must not be edited or altered from its original content. In other words, using the fast forward button is acceptable, but editing or shortening the program tape is not always legal, especially if it removes the copyright information.

As your librarian or technologist accepts taping requests from teachers, keep one requirement in mind: The same teacher may not record, or request to be recorded, the same program multiple times, no matter how many times the program is rebroadcast.

How does one protect oneself and the school from inadvertent infringement in this area?

- Create and maintain a log of recording and use requests. This database will contain a history of all off air recordings used by a particular teacher. While it is possible to manually log recordings, a computer database is the most efficient method of maintaining this type of record.

- Create fields for teacher, program, channel or network, broadcast date or date recorded, and retention rights. When a teacher submits another recording request (or presents a home-recorded video), sort the database on the teacher's name and check earlier requests. It will be easy to find duplication by that teacher.

- Remember that this database will grow. It isn't a database that can be trashed at the end of each school year. Recordings are cumulative. Once a teacher has recorded a particular program (meaning episode or single broadcast), that teacher may not record the same program for class again without express permission, even if the program is rebroadcast many months or years later.

Retention

Once a program is taped, when must you use it? The legal restrictions on retention are extremely strict. A taped program may be kept for a maximum of 45 consecutive (calendar) days. Of those 45 days, students may view the program only during the first 10 school days. (Note that student use considers school days, but total time counts consecutive days, including weekends and holidays.) Even those first 10 days are prescribed: once for instruction, once for review. No other viewings are possible under the fair use guidelines. During the remaining days of the 45-day period, the program may be used only for evaluation of the program by teachers. The program may be retained beyond the 45-day period only if explicit, written permission has been received from the copyright holders. Lacking such permission, the tape must be erased or destroyed at the end of the 45-day period.

Note that these so-called "fair use" rules apply only to programs taped off regular broadcast channels. Cable or satellite programs that permit limited school use may impose specific retention restrictions that may be more liberal or narrower than the standard 10/45-day fair use, e.g. three days, one year, or life-of-tape. Check program guides and cable-in-education periodicals for specific details on each program.

Home recording

It makes no difference where the program was recorded. What affects school use of recorded television programming is the source of the broadcast (broadcast, cable, or satellite) and the date of the recording. The best way to monitor this is to require a signed affidavit stating the date and channel from which the program was recorded. The 10/45-day rules apply to recordings from regular broadcast channels, no matter who makes the recording or where it is recorded. In other words, if a teacher records a program in December, but wants to show it in May, such a showing would not be permitted under fair use, and specific, written permission from the copyright holder would be required.

Copies of off-air recordings

In some cases, one program might be appropriate for more than one class at a time; for example, a documentary might be suitable for all the American history classes to view. In such an instance, the school may make copies of the off-air taping, one for each classroom that would need to view the program at the same time. Each copy must have the same off-air taping notices and copyright information attached, and each copy is subject to the same time restrictions as the original.

Recording in anticipation

Persons in authority may not forecast that teachers will request copies of a particular resource and cause that item to be copied so it will be available on the chance that a teacher might ask for it. This type of situation frequently occurs when a principal or librarian notices that there is a television program scheduled to air that would relate to some curriculum. The educator decides to record the program in expectation that teachers will ask for the program after the fact. In order to comply with the fair use guidelines, the request for recording must come from the teacher who wishes to use the program. This is often described as a "bottom up" rule: The person at the point of use (the classroom) is the one who must make the request for recording.

Public performance rights

Since many audiovisual materials may be purchased with public performance rights, wise administrators ask their librarians to track which of their materials have such rights. Entries in the library catalog, stickers on individual items, and log books all successfully inform library patrons of the items for which rights have been purchased. A notation on how the rights were acquired would be helpful, as well as the duration of the rights, e.g., "via catalog," "life-of-tape," or "on P.O. #123456, 2 years (exp. 11-15-05)."

A file of performance rights documentation would also be a good idea. A few suppliers, especially video producers, provide blanket public performance rights in the prices of all videos in their catalogs. A photocopy of this statement from the catalog attached to the purchase order for the videos should be sufficient documentation. Another supplier includes a statement on the order envelope stating, "The video recordings you purchase from XYZ Company are sold for school and library use. Broadcast rights are not included. Programs may not be reproduced, copied, or transmitted without written permission." An extra-thorough method of ensuring a complete understanding would be to include a line on the purchase order stating: "All materials to include public performance rights" (or archival rights). Acceptance of the order with this statement included would contractually obligate the supplier to provide public performance rights as well.

> **Caveat:** Be certain that you are sending the order to a company that is able to broker such licenses. Some AV jobbers will supply the tapes or DVDs on the purchase order even though they are not able to broker the performance rights. Ask before you order.

The sale of public performance rights is a contractual obligation, so the purchaser and the copyright owner (usually through a supplier or distributor) can negotiate whatever rights package the owner would like to sell and the purchaser can afford. Don't be afraid to propose the type of performance rights you need. The worst the copyright owner can do is say "no." Just make sure you prepare your proposal far in advance of your anticipated performance date. The educational fair use exemptions don't apply to public performances and if you have not acquired the necessary rights before your public performance, you are on extremely hazardous ground.

Archiving audiovisual works

Copyright law pertaining to computer software allows the purchaser to make a single backup copy (also called archival copy) of the medium in case something unfortunate should happen to the originals. Unfortunately, audiovisual materials do not offer the same archival permission. Owners of film, video, or audio may not make backup copies of the works. The usual terms of purchase are similar to that of a book: you may use the material until it wears out or breaks. At that point you may attempt to repair it, but the best alternative is to replace the work. In the case of video and audio, this is called "life of tape (this term is used even for material on other media, such as DVD and CD).

CLOSED CAPTIONING

There has been much discussion of the legality of adding closed captions to existing video. Some experts argue that adding the special digital coding required for this feature results in a "derivative work" (Sinofsky, 1993; Kruppenbacher, 1993). Such a derivative work would not be in compliance with copyright. Kruppenbacher, ITV program coordinator at the National Technical Institute for the Deaf, argues that, in order to make a closed-captioned copy, one must make a working copy to which one adds the necessary encoding. He contends that the working copy is, in itself, a violation of copyright.

However, Congressman Robert Kastenmeier stated during congressional arguments on the Copyright Revision Act of 1976 that the legislative intent of the law would specifically allow the making of a working copy with closed captioning in an institution serving the hearing impaired, as long as the copy stayed within the institution requiring it. The copy must necessarily be restricted from general use, but it might be shared among other institutions serving hearing-impaired populations (Official Fair Use Guidelines, 1987, p.17).

Such diverse opinions put use of this technology in the gray area. If your building has a population of hearing-impaired patrons, you would probably be safe in closed-captioning your videos that aren't already so encoded. Keep in mind the guidelines Congressman Kastenmeier set forth as parameters and you will probably not be challenged. If still in doubt, consult a copyright attorney.

VIDEO DISTRIBUTION

Video distribution is a type of closed-circuit network in which a classroom teacher (usually) controls video being sent from centralized equipment in the building. Videos are loaded into centrally housed players and are either started at a predetermined time or are started by the particular teacher requesting the program. The software that controls the players can track and record usage and generate reports of which recordings and players were used most often, and which recordings were played by which teachers.

In-house video streaming setups can often perform the same functions. The primary disadvantage is that the person loading and perhaps starting the videos becomes a part of the copyright compliance loop.

According to Mary Brandt Jensen, law professor, the person loading and starting the programs can be considered a contributory infringer if "the [person] caused, assisted, encouraged, or authorized the patron to do the infringing act or was in a position to control the use of the copyrighted work by the patron" (Jensen, 1992, p. 150).

The author solved the problem of questionable videotapes in the video distribution system by requesting certain documents from teachers before the tapes were played:

- If the recording to be played is owned by the library, all the teacher need submit is a copy of the lesson plan showing the link between the lesson and the video.

- If the recording to be shown was rented from a local video store, the teacher still must meet the fair use requirements of the law in order to use the recording in class.

- If the program was recorded off-air, the teacher must submit a verification of fair use compliance.

Recording off-air, in contrast to recording from cable, is permissible within strict fair-use guidelines. Those guidelines were discussed in the section on off-air recording. Programs recorded by the library staff at the request of teachers should be clearly labeled as copyrighted material, and both the record date and erase date explicitly noted on the recording.

Administrators can make a modest effort to protect themselves and their schools by requesting disclosure forms from persons wishing to play video through the centralized system. With such verification on file, the school should have a modicum of protection if the tape is later found to be out of compliance.

DIGITAL VIDEO SERVERS

When converting analog (tape) videos into digital (hard disk) storage, one must first convert the format of the video. Format conversion is an adaptation, creating a derivative work. This is a violation of one of the rights of the copyright holder. In addition, the purpose of the conversion is to distribute the video, another right of the copyright holder. Naturally, you have also made a copy of the work, and you have copied all of it. The work is creative, and you have done the copying to avoid paying for a digital copy of the work. So a fair use assessment here doesn't look good either. Use extreme caution in making these conversions.

Sound recordings

Sound recordings, as used in this section, will include phonograph records, cassette tapes in analog and digital formats, compact discs, reel-to-reel tape, and hard disk-based recordings. These are distinct from the section on music because music also includes the print music notation, as well as performance of the printed music. This section will only deal with recorded aspects of music, but will also include all other types of recordings, such as spoken word.

All the formats listed above can be and are copyrighted. Even if you do not see a copyright symbol on the item itself, you must assume all materials to be copyrighted unless specifically shown otherwise because the law no longer requires notice of copyright. Some recordings use the special symbol assigned to phonorecords–a "p" in a circle, similar to the "c" in a circle commonly understood to be the symbol designating copyrighted print materials. Remember that neither symbol is required.

Recordings fixed prior to February 15, 1972 may have had some copyright protection under state copyright laws, but such protection is highly variable.

Since the Internet has become an active medium in the transmission of sound recordings, and because many people are substituting Internet transmissions of performances for the purchase of CDs, in 1995 Congress granted public performance rights to "digital audio performances." Web pages that deliver recordings on the request of the viewer may be in violation of the new right (17 U.S.C. §§ 114(d-f)). The No Electronic Theft (NET) Act (P.L. 105-147) provides criminal penalties for those who violate copyright of sound recordings via the Internet, even if the violator makes no profit from the exchange. (Recording Industry Association of America, 2003).

Sound recordings have the same requirements and permissions as do all audiovisual materials. Sound recordings of music add an extra onus to the mix. A work may involve three copyrights: one for the music itself, a second for the recording, and a third on the arrangement. For example, a current hit record may have music and lyrics copyrighted by the author, while the actual recording of the performance of that music and lyrics may be covered by an entirely different copyright. In order to receive permission to use the recording in any derivative work, videotape, or public performance, you must get permission from all copyright holders. Occasionally a teacher will ask students to perform music and record the performance to use as background music for a multimedia presentation. Even if the music is in the public domain, the arrangement of the music may not be. Additionally, the students now own the copyright to their own performance of the music. Clearance will be required for any use beyond use by the students involved. Two organizations do most of the copyright clearances for professional music recordings: American Society of Composers, Authors and Publishers (ASCAP, <www.ascap.com>) and Broadcast Music Inc. (BMI, <www.bmi.com>).

As with all audiovisual materials, the owner of a copy of a sound recording may not make any copies of the original, even archival copies. Some tapes may be purchased with duplication rights, especially foreign language tapes. Be sure to retain the paperwork granting the duplication rights and any restrictions that may accompany them, e.g., duplication of one copy per student or one copy per textbook purchased. If such numerical restrictions apply, create and maintain a log of duplications. A bit of extra time spent in the process can save many hours of research compiling records at a later date, should you be challenged on compliance.

Sampling

The amazing capabilities of digital editing equipment make all sorts of creative work with audio not only possible but also simple. This equipment is so sophisticated that individual wave forms can be edited, copied, modified, or erased. The technology is called "sampling." Several lawsuits have been filed and won as a result of one party extracting selected sounds from a copyrighted work and inserting them into a new, derivative work.

How much sampling is "too much" in a fair use assessment? A copyright attorney posted on CNI-COPYRIGHT that if a consumer can recognize a snippet of a song as being from the original, that is too much.

The MP3 dilemma

As the Napster case (A&M Records, Inc. v Napster, Inc., 284 F.3d 1091 (C.A.9 (Cal.),2002)) has shown, some trading of copyright-protected material via file sharing networks is illegal. Schools will want to watch for packets associated with various file sharing software packages since the Recording Industry Association of America (RIAA) has declared its intent to sue educational institutions for contributory and/or vicarious infringement if shared files are traced back to those organizations. The RIAA declares: "A copyright is infringed when a song is made available to the public by uploading it to an Internet site for other people to download, sending it through an email or chat service, or otherwise reproducing or distributing copies without authorization from the copyright owner. In civil cases copyright infringement can occur whether or not money was exchanged for the music, and in criminal cases there only needs to be a possibility of financial loss to the copyright holder or financial gain to the infringer. The NET Act sets penalties for willful copyright infringement" (RIAA, 2003).

The NET Act imposes criminal penalties of up to five years in prison, and fines up to $250,000 in statutory fines if the infringement included an expectation of financial gain. That expectation could be as little as expecting another file in return, as is the case with file sharing.

RESOURCE SHARING

Audiovisual materials that are licensed and not purchased may be restricted from lending to other schools. Even listing these in the library catalog or list of available materials can violate the license if no loans to outside buildings are permitted. Read the license to know what rights you purchased.

CHAPTER 6

Music Materials in Schools (print and recorded)

M usic, as with most of the other media, has its own set of guidelines. Music, in the context used here, means sheet music, not sound recordings. However, making sound recordings of sheet music will fall under these guidelines in certain circumstances.

WHAT TYPICAL ACTIVITIES ARE COVERED?

Typical activities in schools include reproduction and performance to some extent. Keep in mind that printed music is always covered by the print guidelines. However, certain uses of music in education are exempt from the print requirements in ways that standard prose is not.

Reproduction of sheet music–issues

Sheet music publishers make their livelihood from selling copies of sheet music. With photocopiers able to make fast, high-quality copies, this method of piracy is a serious threat to music publishers.

Performances of sheet music–issues

Even if students are expected to memorize music before performance, the music being played originated with sheet music. Performances of music beyond the classroom are public performances. However, for non-dramatic performances in school where there is no admission charged, or where all of the admission proceeds go to the educational institution, most use is permitted unless the copyright owner objects at least seven days in advance.

Reproduction of recorded music–issues

Occasionally music teachers need to make copies of recorded music for their students. Teachers may make copies of complete works or portions of works, and may make anthologies of such excerpts **only** for the purpose of conducting "aural exercises or examinations."

Performances of recorded music–issues

Performing recorded, copyright-protected sheet music is a common occurrence. Most of these issues are addressed in the chapter on audiovisual materials under the section on sound recording. However, some additional topics come into play. Non-instructional public performances of recorded music always require a license. The difficulty is in getting a license for a secondary or elementary school.

Adaptation of sheet music–issues

All adaptations are within the rights of the copyright owner. However, schools do have some limited exemptions to create adapted works within an educational context.

WHAT GUIDELINES AFFECT MUSIC?

There is no section of current copyright law that identifies specific guidelines for permitted educational uses of music, either printed or recorded. However, several groups collaborated to draw up a set of guidelines that address the unique aspects of using music in schools. In 1976, at the same time Congress was developing the Fair Use Guidelines, several music industry groups and music educators developed the Guidelines for Educational Uses of Music and submitted them to the Congressional committee considering educational guidelines. The Committee agreed that the guidelines were reasonable, and endorsed them. Since these guidelines aren't law, they are more of a "gentlemen's agreement" than believing that the uses described are acceptable by all parties.

In addition, standard tests of fair use always apply, as may the print guidelines, audiovisual guidelines, TEACH act, and multimedia guidelines. Always look at all aspects of a given situation to assess all the possible angles before making a determination if a use is fair or not.

There are actually three sets of guidelines covering educational use of music. The longer lived of the guidelines, The Guidelines for Educational Uses of Music, are generally accepted. Following guidelines promulgated by such a collaborative group (composed of copyright owners and end users) forms a reasonable basis to make decisions on what types of use are appropriate. Beyond what these guidelines offer, the Music Publisher's Association has some additional guidelines, as does the National Association for Music Education. Both these supplemental guidelines expand on the original set of rules, and add supplemental information on new technologies that were not available when the original guidelines were written in 1976. The expansions are not endorsed by copyright owner groups, however, so use caution in their application.

PRINT MUSIC

The types of copying of printed music that are acceptable include:

- Emergency copying when purchased copies have not arrived in time for a performance, with the understanding that the emergency copies will be replaced with purchased copies.

- For non-performance classroom purposes, the teacher may make one or more copies of portions of works, as long as the parts are not a part that would constitute a "performable unit such as a section, movement or aria." The copied portion may not exceed 10 percent of the whole work. You may only make one copy per pupil.

- If the school buys sufficient copies of printed music, those copies may be edited or simplified as long as the fundamental character of the work is not changed (e.g. jazz stays jazz), or the lyrics are not altered or added if none exist.

According to the guidelines, there are several prohibited types of music copying:

- Any copying that substitutes for purchasing a compilation, anthology, or collection of music.

- Any copying of "consumable" materials such as workbooks, tests, exercises, etc.

- Copying music for performance, except as explained in the first permission above.

- Copying with the intention of not purchasing music, except as explained in the first and second permissions above.

- Copying without including the copyright notice that appears on the printed copy.

Recorded music

Under certain circumstances school users may make copies of recorded music. Those circumstances include:

- You may make a single copy of recordings of performances by students but it may only be used for evaluation or rehearsal. This recording may be kept by the school or individual teacher.

- You may make a single copy of a sound recording of copyrighted music (as long as the recording is owned by the school or an individual teacher) for the purpose of constructing "aural exercises or examinations." This derivative recording may be retained by the school or teacher. (This permission pertains only to the copyright of the printed music and not to any copyright which may exist in the sound recording.)

What rules/laws are different about recordings?

Recordings are treated no differently if they are music than if they are spoken word. **The five yes/no tests still apply to using copyrighted recordings of music in the classroom** (see page 49-50). The direct teaching aspect will be an essential element of the fair use assessment, so entertainment, ambience, or enrichment are not sufficient to get the nod on the face-to-face teaching question. The bad news about using sound recordings is that two copyrights apply to sound recordings created after February 1, 1972. Prior to 1972, there was no copyright in the actual recording, so a recording of public domain music (such as much of classical music) would be in the public domain. After 1972, however, there is a copyright in the underlying composition (sheet music) plus a copyright in the recorded performance. For that reason, recent recordings of Bach, Beethoven, and the great masters (in fact, any music published before 1923 as long as it is in the original form) are protected by copyright even though the underlying work is long in the public domain.

A hot topic in the recording industry today involves peer-to-peer file sharing. Individual users, for private use, may make copies of works they lawfully own. So someone might copy a song from a compact disc to an MP3 player in a completely lawful manner. However, schools are not individual users, and making copies of recordings must follow the requirements set forth above. Sharing digital files with others who do not own legal copies of recordings is not legal, for both individual users and schools. In addition, the RIAA announced its intention to sue those who enable users to share software (ITVibe, 2004). If peer-to-peer file sharing software is installed on school computers, and users distribute a significant amount of music, the host and the individual may be named in suits.

MUSIC IN PERFORMANCE

Performing music can happen in a classroom setting, or it can happen in a public performance such as a concert, sports event, talent show, dance recital, musical or other event. Some key questions to ask when assessing potential for liability in music performance include:

- Is the work a musical, opera, operetta, or other dramatic work? Dramatic works have no exemptions under the guidelines, and permission from a rights holder or broker is always required, even for no-charge performances.

- Is the performance part of face-to-face teaching? Following the audiovisual guidelines, the five yes/no tests give guidance in the appropriate setting to use music.

- Is the performance live, with no commercial advantage? This strange phrase means that no performers, promoters, or organizers get any money from the event, and that there is no direct or indirect admission charge (Althouse, 1999, p. 75). There is a small exception for this rule, however. If all proceeds go to educational, religious or charitable purposes, an admission fee is acceptable. However, making copies of the performance to sell would not be within the limits since it is beyond a live performance.

PERFORMANCE RIGHTS ORGANIZATIONS

Suppose you have determined that you need permission or license to copy or arrange music, to have a dance with a DJ, or to perform music where the performers are paid though the proceeds will go to the booster club or the PTA. A performing rights organization will be a convenient place to get those rights. None of the major rights organizations offer a campus or district license for K-12 education. With such a license a school would be able to play music on the telephone, offer background music in the lunchroom, perform music at athletic events, and hire a local band to perform for the student dance.

A blanket license that covers everything on the campus is not the only way to comply with the law, however. For example, if the band boosters should decide to hire a local band to perform a concert to raise money for new band instruments, a school would need to contact one of the organizations for a single performance license in order to be within the limitations of the law (Althouse, 1999, 83).

PERMISSIONS

To get permission to make new arrangements of music, to translate or adapt music, to perform music in a broadcast setting, or any of the many other times that exemptions do not cover the activities in a school, one should contact either the rights broker or the copyright owner for permission. When requesting permission, it is important to be explicit in what you plan to do, how many times, how many copies, what use will be made of the resulting material. The publisher or copyright owner is not required to reply to your request.

Depending on what you want to do will depend on the type of license or permission you need. Public performances and copying sheet music need permissions from ASCAP or BMI. If you plan to record sheet music (such as making copies of a band or choir performance), you need what is known as a "mechanical license" from the Harry Fox Agency <www.harryfox.com > (Music Publishers' Association, 2004). The Music Publishers' Association has several useful forms for requesting permission or license to copy or perform music on their Web site <www.mpa.org>.

CHAPTER 7

Multimedia in Schools

M ultimedia was invented after the latest revision of copyright law. There are no definitive court cases in this arena, but thanks to the hard work of a group of media producers, publishers, and media consumers, a set of clear-cut industry-developed guidelines on the use of multimedia in education was approved late in 1996.

MULTIMEDIA GUIDELINES

When multimedia first emerged as an educational medium, there were no copyright rules that addressed the types of uses required for the technology. Falling back on the print guidelines, or the audiovisual guidelines just didn't address the unique needs of this technology. In order to create a multimedia work, virtually all the relevant material must be transferred to digital format. Music, video or still images, and graphics all have different copyrights. And while you may own a CD recording, for example, all you really own is the right to listen to the music until the disk breaks or wears out. You don't own the rights to convert any of that material into another format such as a computer disk or DVD.

In order to clarify exactly what uses of traditional media would be considered "fair" in this new technology, the Conference on Fair Use (CONFU) set about to gather potential stakeholders to negotiate fair use guidelines for several different areas of electronic access, including multimedia. These guidelines outline the limits of acceptable use of copyrighted materials in fair use situations. The guidelines are not law, just as the classroom guidelines are not law. The guidelines are simply an agreement between those who own the copyrights and those who wish to use the copyrighted materials on what will be permitted under a claim of fair use. Compliance under the guidelines doesn't mean the use is "legal." It means that the copyright holder agrees not to sue someone who uses their materials within these limits.

The agreement on **Fair Use Guidelines for Educational Multimedia** provides concrete limits on the types and amounts of material that may be included in works created by teachers and students. One of the first notations in the guidelines is that all materials used in derivative works should be properly cited as being taken from the works of others. The guidelines also state that multimedia works made from the copyrighted materials of others may be used only in support of the education of students in nonprofit educational institutions.

 Special definitions for multi-media

Educational institutions: "nonprofit organizations whose primary focus is supporting research and instructional activities of educators and students for noncommercial purposes" (Educational Multimedia Fair Use Guidelines Development Committee, 1997).

Educational multimedia projects: Programs that "incorporate students' or educators' original material, such as course notes or commentary, together with various copyrighted media formats including but not limited to, motion media, music, text material, graphics, illustrations, photographs and digital software which are combined into an integrated presentation" (Educational Multimedia Fair Use Guidelines Development Committee, 1997).

Educational purposes: "systematic learning activities including use in connection with non-commercial curriculum-based learning and teaching activities by educators to students enrolled in courses at nonprofit educational institutions" (Educational Multimedia Fair Use Guidelines Development Committee, 1997).

Educators: "faculty, teachers, instructors, and others who engage in scholarly research and instructional activities for educational institutions" (Educational Multimedia Fair Use Guidelines Development Committee, 1997).

Lawfully acquired: "obtained by the institution or individual through lawful means such as purchase, gift or license agreement but not pirated copies" (Educational Multimedia Fair Use Guidelines Development Committee, 1997).

Multimedia: "Material is stored so that it may be retrieved in a nonlinear fashion, depending on the needs or interests of learners" (Educational Multimedia Fair Use Guidelines Development Committee, 1997).

Multimedia–covered or not?

All references to multimedia works are to productions that include copyrighted materials. Obviously, any multimedia production in which the teacher or student creates all the text, data, sounds, and graphics would be totally under the control of the creator. The guidelines permit multimedia works made by students to be used in the class for which they were created, and also retained in portfolios *maintained by the student* for job interviews, college applications, and other purposes. Teachers may use the multimedia presentations they create in face-to-face instruction, or they may assign students to view the presentations on their own. Repeatedly in the guidelines, you see the phrase "Educator Use for Curriculum-Based Instruction." The guidelines are very much in the same vein as the audiovisual guidelines and the print guidelines in that they support direct teaching but not the supplemental, extracurricular activities so often seen in schools.

Retention and access

Teachers may display their own multimedia programs at conferences and work-shops, and they may retain the programs they create in portfolios for job interviews, evaluations, and other uses. There is a finite limit to an educator's right to keep a work created from copyrighted material, however. While a student may keep a work indefinitely, a teacher may keep a work for only two years from the time of its first use with a class. Beyond the two-year window, permission to retain or use the material is required for **each** portion of copyrighted material used in the presentation

If a multimedia work is to be used on a network several factors come into play. To ensure that only students enrolled in the course may see the program, some type of security is required. Students must log in or provide some other evidence of identity. In addition, the network over which the program is transmitted must have in place a means to prohibit copying of the program, such as encryption or other copy protection technology. If there is no such safeguard, the program may be used on the network for only 15 days. After that time, the program disk may be checked out to students, but only with a warning that the program may not be copied.

Quantity limits

The guidelines specify the amounts of different types of copyrighted materials from a single source that may be used in all multimedia projects created in the course of a term. In other words, from any one video, recording, or database, a specific limit is assigned that a student or teacher may not exceed in a single year or term. Should a teacher reach this theoretical limit, any additional material in a presentation would require permission.

The multimedia guideline limits are:

- **Motion media (film, video, television):** Up to 10 percent or three minutes, whichever is less, of an individual program.

- **Text (prose, poetry, drama):** Up to 10 percent or 1,000 words, whichever is less, of a novel, story, play, or long poem. Short poems less than 250 words may be used in their entirety. Only three poems by one poet or five poems by different poets from an anthology may be used. For poems longer than 250 words, only three excerpts from one poet or five from works by different poets in an anthology are permitted.

- **Music, lyrics, and music video:** Up to 10 percent but not more than 30 seconds from a single work (or combined from separate extracts of a work).

- **Illustrations, cartoons, and photographs:** A work may be used in its entirety but only if no more than five images from a single artist or photographer are used in a multimedia work. In addition, if images are taken from a single collective work, no more than 10 percent or 15 images may be used.

- **Numerical data sets** (computer databases or spreadsheets): Up to 10 percent or 2,500 fields or cells, whichever is less, may be used from a copyrighted database.

How many copies?

An educator or student may make only two copies (including the original) of the multimedia work. An additional copy may be made if one of the copies is lost, stolen, or damaged. If more than one person creates the multimedia work, each may have one copy of the work. Each copy may be retained as long as is permitted for the type of author (student or teacher).

Other restrictions

The opening screen of the multimedia work and any accompanying printed materials must contain a notice that the work contains copyrighted materials that have been used under the fair use exemption of the U.S. Copyright Law. While the guidelines don't specify the wording of the notice, something like the following would meet the requirement:

NOTICE: The following presentation contains copyrighted materials used under the Multimedia Guidelines and Fair Use exemptions of U.S. Copyright law. Further use is prohibited.

NOTICE (for young students): I borrowed other people's stuff to create my project. I followed the rules. Please don't copy my project.

Attribution

The guidelines and academic integrity require complete attribution and acknowledgment of all copyright protected materials used in a multimedia presentation. In a multimedia presentation, at the point of insertion of some external, copyright protected work (video, image, audio, etc.) include a shorthand reference to that item as listed in the complete Works Cited section. The type of reference can be consistent with whatever style sheet governs the project.

In addition to the in-text attribution, the multimedia guidelines require specific information in the entries in the Works Cited section. The items that must be included are:

- Author
- Title
- Publisher
- Place of publication

- Date of publication
- Copyright symbol (©)
- Year of first publication
- Name of the copyright holder

Think of a multimedia project as a research paper, with a short citation at the point of use directing the viewer to a complete citation in the mediagraphy.

Best Advice: Invest in clip art, music, and video sold expressly for multimedia productions, or create your own. The multimedia collections are always copyright cleared for such applications. Clip art **books** would fall under the "illustrations" portion of the guidelines, since one would have to scan or otherwise digitize the images to include them in a multimedia presentation.

CHAPTER 8

Distance Learning in Schools

Distance learning has been a black eye for copyright advocates for a long time. A significant reason is that Congress has a hard time keeping up with the pace of technological change. Add to that the age of most congressmen and senators, and you realize that they just don't understand how distance learning works, much less how the use of copyrighted material is just as essential to the success of distance learning as it is to face-to-face instruction. To provide guidance in this area, Congress passed the TEACH Act, which identifies copyright guidelines for distance learning.

TEACH ACT

The TEACH Act provides considerable support for using copyright protected audio and video materials in online and video distributed courses as long as they are used in support of direct instruction. The act requires several conditions to be met before the protections of the act are available. Following the lead of the audiovisual Guidelines, the TEACH Act requires:

- A direct connection to the current curriculum.
- That only officially registered students may view the materials.

- That both the transmitting and receiving ends of a transmission must see that transient copies of works are removed quickly (by flushing the cache, etc.).

- That the transmitting body is responsible to protect the copyright of any materials it transmits. (This means the school is ultimately responsible for protecting any copyrighted materials it uses in distance learning.)

In order to make the law as forward-looking as possible, the act isn't restricted to the types of distance learning that existed at the time of the passage. Rather, the teaching activity as a whole must meet the definition of "distance education" as defined in the law:

- Must occur in discrete installments
- Must occur within a confined span of time (undefined)
- Parts must integrate into a "lecture-like" whole
- "Mediated instructional activities" must resemble traditional classroom sessions.

These activities are expressly prohibited by the TEACH Act:

- Scanning or uploading complete or long works
- Storing works on open Web sites (no login/password)
- Allowing student access at will (such as supplemental material, or material with no specific, limited time frame)

Three groups share statutory responsibility for complying with the requirements of the TEACH Act: policymakers, information technology staff, and instructors/developers. Each group has specific tasks assigned, and unless all three groups do their part, the protections of the act fall away. Compliance must be a carefully considered, well-orchestrated activity.

POLICYMAKERS

Policymakers are, in most instances, the board of education. This group must be able to verify nonprofit educational status. Generally the state education agency can certify a district's status, but other methods are possible. The board must have an adopted copyright policy. Faculty, students, and staff must be trained on copyright compliance.

The policymakers must order that access to distance learning materials is limited to enrolled students only. Restricting access to enrolled students resembles the audiovisual guidelines' directive that only students and teachers in a class be present when copyrighted audiovisuals are shown under a fair use defense. If your district offers self-enrollment for community education classes, such access would prohibit the use of copyrighted materials under the protections of TEACH.

INFORMATION TECHNOLOGY STAFF

The information technology (IT) staff bears a significant part of the burden of compliance with TEACH Act provisions. They must assure that only registered students can access course materials. They must prevent students from capturing material for longer than a class session. Preventing capture may mean encrypting materials, in some cases. The IT staff must prevent student redistribution of copyrighted material. Preventing redistribution may go hand-in-hand with preventing capture, if streaming technologies are used.

IT staff must protect digital rights management information, which can include verifying that materials have not been cropped or edited to remove copyright notices, and that all audiovisual materials include credits and copyright statements. They must make sure only "intended recipients" can access any transmissions. This requirement will require working with internetwork hosts, if any, to see that access to files and data streams are secure.

Finally, the IT staff must make long-term retention out of student reach. Copyrighted works may be retained from term to term, for example, but they must be stored in access areas that are not available to students or others. This requirement is particularly important for programs where online or broadcast courses are hosted on remote servers or through remote transmission facilities. The IT staff must see that the courses are taken offline, and stored where the staff at the hosting facility can't access the copyright protected materials.

INSTRUCTORS/DEVELOPERS

Instructors and developers of courses and course materials bear the biggest burden in TEACH Act compliance. Regarding copyrighted materials they may include in a course, they may read stories, poems, essays, etc. They may play non dramatic music (not musicals or operas). An instructor may show "reasonable and limited" portions of dramatic audiovisual works (movies and operas). The term "reasonable and limited" is given no specific time period, however, in a face-to-face class a teacher may show an entire film, if that film meets the audiovisual guidelines tests. The act goes on to state that the teacher may use other works typical of a classroom session.

An instructor may not (under fair use) use any work marketed for online learning, such as digital curriculum, electronic databases, or learning systems. All online learning materials are licensed for online learning, and using these materials under fair use would deprive the copyright owner of a sale of a license for these materials. In addition, an instructor or developer may not use anything that is from an illegal copy if he had any reason to think the copy might be illegal. So using a

DVD that was purchased from a video supplier, and that comes in an appropriate looking case, would not raise any suspicions that the product was manufactured in the far East in a pirate facility. The user would likely be exempt from liability in such a situation.

An instructor must:

- Plan and conduct all use of copyrighted materials
- Insure that all use is part of regular, systematic instruction
- Insure that all use is directly related to teaching content
- Insure that all use is not entertainment, reward, or enrichment

An instructor or designer may digitize materials if the use meets portion limitations. In addition, the instructor must verify that no digital version of the work is available or that the work is inaccessible because of a protection scheme.

Finally, the instructor may not digitize textbooks, books, workbooks, etc. Students or schools are expected to purchase books and workbooks in the traditional manner. Some occasional handouts are likely okay in the manner of the original print guidelines.

Many school activities will fall under the TEACH Act's provisions even if the school isn't teaching complete courses online. Many teachers use a Web site for course support, or to mount today's homework worksheet in case it "gets lost" on the way home. School or library Web pages may use copyright protected materials in pursuit of their educational goals, but don't qualify for the special exemptions permitted under TEACH. A careful analysis of the situation will determine if the TEACH Act provisions may be relied upon for a given situation.

C HAPTER 9

Internet in Schools

Internet is the latest communication medium. It is only natural that this would be a widely used communications channel in schools. However, on the Internet you are on your own, copyright-wise. There are no Internet-specific guidelines to regulate our activities.

WHAT TYPICAL ACTIVITIES ARE COVERED?

Because the Internet is so broad in its coverage and style, the types of activities that fall into this area are huge:

- *Printing pages:* Printing pages from the Internet falls under similar rules to those of the print guidelines. Look to those for how many copies one may make and what one may do with them.

- *Links:* Links can be problematic when the Web page owner objects to your link to their page. The primary reason the owner might object is that they feel you are capitalizing on their site without appropriate attribution or payment. Using frames to access a Web site hides the true origin of a Web page (the URL doesn't show in the address bar) and the actual Web site from which the content is displayed may get no acknowledgement. While individual links may be public domain facts, collections of links, especially those collections with significant organization or annotation, gain what is called a "compilation copyright" over the selection, annotation, and organization of those links. Web site owners also object to "deep links"–links into pages within the site that by using them the user bypasses splash screens, links to other products, and advertising on which the Web site owner relies for income.

- *Copying pages to local servers:* When Internet access is slow, or a large number of students must access the same material at once, it is sometimes easier to copy a Web page or Web site and put the information on a local server rather than bringing the page across the Internet every time a student must get information. Some software will allow you to copy an entire site at once, even collecting outside pages or sites to which the first page is linked. Going through a fair use assessment doesn't provide much support that copying this extensively and then redistributing would be a fair use.

- *Redistributing pages:* Copying a page is not the only potential troublespot for appropriating Web material. Sometimes teachers or students not only copy material from a Web page, but they also incorporate that material into a new page. Once the new page has been mounted on the Web, it has been distributed to the world, violating the original author's right of distribution.

- *Email:* Email is probably the most abused Internet property. It is forwarded, edited, copied, and reprinted, sometimes to the point that the original author is long lost. Email, as with other written material, is the intellectual property of its author if the contents of the email are minimally creative. Because an email is not published (it is a private communication, just as a letter is), protection for email is much stronger than for typical published materials. The recipient may retain his one copy of the email, but he may not redistribute it, adapt it, or make additional copies of the email without permission.

- *Chat and IM:* Chat and instant messenger applications are blocked in many schools, but for those that allow the practice, the communications in both of those applications are usually ephemeral–they exist only briefly and are not saved "in tangible form." When a work is not fixed in tangible form, no copyright exists. However, if the chat is logged or archived, each participant would own the rights to his respective contributions.

SPECIAL RULES FOR THE INTERNET

The Digital Millennium Copyright Act established some forms of protection from liability that may affect schools. Detailed in Section 512, the many specific requirements to be eligible for protection under this section are quite complex. Essentially, the law states that if an Internet (or online) service provider registers with the Copyright Office, and if they comply with a long string of action items–such as agreeing to remove potentially infringing material once it is brought to their attention–the copyright infringement exposure of the online service provider (OSP) is limited. Schools, because they provide Internet access to their staff and students, are probably OSPs or Internet service providers (ISPs). The protection offered by the DMCA only extends to the school or district, not to the individuals who may have committed the infringements.

Registered agent

The designation of someone to be the copyright agent for notification of claims of copyright infringement is one step that schools can easily take. The school designates a single person who will respond to claims of copyright infringement and registers that person with the Copyright Office (<http://www.copyright.gov/onlinesp/>). The school posts complete contact information for this person on the school Web site. If someone should find infringing material on a Web page, he notifies the copyright agent, who will then take down or disable access to the material in question.

By complying with the requirements of the Digital Millennium Copyright Act OSP provisions, the school is protected against liability for infringements that may happen as a result of students or teachers posting infringing materials on a school Web site. Having a registered agent, and following the appropriate take down provisions, the school is protected from a lawsuit (though the busted student is now in the hot seat).

WHAT GUIDELINES AFFECT THE INTERNET?

There are no set copyright guidelines for the Internet. Because the Internet is composed of print, music, audiovisuals, multimedia, and computer software, none of the established guidelines fit perfectly but ALL of the established guidelines may apply to some extent. For that reason, it is often easier to fall back on the standard four fair use questions (see page 24) to determine if the use of material taken from the Internet is fair. Also

> *There are no set copyright guidelines for the Internet. Also remember that access to many of the works on the Internet is through license.*

remember that access to many of the works on the Internet is through license. Articles from online databases and Web sites that require registration predicate access to those items on terms of the license agreement rather than through fair use. Whatever terms you accept through the license are binding, even if those terms are more restrictive than those of fair use or agreed guidelines. The key to knowing what to use is knowing what items on the Internet are protected by copyright.

Suppose you write a document on a word processor. Perhaps it is a poem or a chapter of a book. As soon as you save the file on the hard disk, your work is protected under copyright. You can send the chapter to your publisher, you can ask other writers to read the manuscript and give suggestions, and you can pass out copies at workshops. The work is still protected under copyright law. Should one of those people take your manuscript and misuse it, you could sue with a reasonable likelihood of success. You may register your work with the Copyright Office if you like, but registration isn't required. Registration does, however, confer a number of important advantages for enforcement.

Now suppose you put that very same manuscript on your Internet homepage. Have you just abandoned the copyright to that work? Not at all. You still own the six rights of a copyright holder: reproduction, distribution, adaptation, public performance, public display, and digital transmission of sound recordings–and so do other creators of materials available via the Internet. And, because the United States is a signatory to the Berne Convention, no notice of copyright is required on **any** item in order for the item to be protected by copyright law.

APPLICATION OF FAIR USE TO INTERNET MATERIALS

Certainly there are some documents that state that they have been dedicated to the public domain, or that use for nonprofit purposes is permitted by the copyright holder. Naturally these situations are apart from the average item located on the Internet. And a case may be made for fair use of Internet materials, just as one may make a claim of fair use for print and audiovisual materials. Similar situations must apply before a claim of fair use may be considered valid. Since there are to this point virtually no significant cases dealing with fair use of Internet materials, one must analyze and evaluate every use in the light of the general guidelines. Remember that each of the four tests of fair use must be weighed against every claim:

- *The purpose of the use:* Is the use for nonprofit educational purposes? Displaying a Web page or making a transparency of some information for the purposes of teaching a lesson at a public or nonprofit private school would likely be looked upon favorably.

- *The character of the use:* What type of material is going to be used? Factual material placed on the Internet has little protection of copyright since facts can't be copyrighted. If you are using lists of common facts such as the 10 longest rivers, or population figures, you have much more latitude to use the material. Highly creative material, such as art work, videos, or Web page design would be much more highly protected.

- *The amount of material copied (also called the extent):* How much of the material are you going to use? If you plan to copy the entire item (whole text file, complete graphic, entire Web page) you'd best have good answers to the other three qualifying questions. The more of an item you plan to use, the less leeway you are permitted. This factor has significant impact on software that can capture entire Web sites for use in an offline situation.

- *The effect of the use on the market for the work:* What effect would your type of use have if everyone made similar use of the material? For example, if everyone were to download the whole Web page, do you think anyone would want to visit the site? Probably not. When you consider that some sites have advertising or other agendas on their sites, they wouldn't want someone to miss seeing those friendly notices. Missing those advertisements would potentially deprive the sponsor of revenue. As far as copyright goes, that is a no-no.

Keep in mind that each classroom use of material retrieved from the Internet must be weighed against these four factors. Imagine a scale, and each of the factors coming onto the scale on either the side for you or the side against you. Some of the factors weigh more than others. The fourth factor, for example, weighs much more than all the others. Consider that when making your analysis.

SPECIAL CONSIDERATIONS FOR DIFFERENT INTERNET SERVICES

The Internet has several unique services that require analysis for appropriate use in a copyright context. Email, news, discussion groups, file transfer (including peer-to-peer file sharing), and the Web all require specific types of analysis.

Email

The author of an email message owns the content of that message. For safe parameters, keep private email private unless you have express permission of the original writer. Don't forward it to newsgroups or listservs, don't include it in a message to a third party, and don't post it on your Web page, unless you receive permission.

Newsgroup and discussion list information

When someone posts a message to a newsgroup or a discussion list, he or she makes an implied decision to "publish" the work. Once a work is published, there is much more latitude to use portions of that work within the fair use exemption. One may, however, negate that implied license simply by noting in the posting that you request the material not be distributed beyond the list. Again, there are no significant court cases to support these assumptions. These are rules derived from the world of print and extrapolated into cyberspace.

For a safe guideline, you can probably copy a few sentences or paragraphs of a newsgroup or discussion list posting since it was published, as long as you aren't going to use it for a money-making purpose. You can also probably repost the article or message to another newsgroup unless the original author states that it isn't permitted. It is always good manners (and safe legal practice) to ask permission to repost.

Use of Web page information

When deciding how to use a Web page, make your analysis similar to a print document or an audiovisual item (depending on what you will be using from the Web). Keep in mind the four tests of fair use. The nonprofit educational use is a given, but what about the character of the material used and the extent of the material used? The more creative the site (i.e., the less factual) the less of the site may be used without prior permission. As a matter of good teaching, use only what is necessary, then get on to other things.

Using any Web page involves a display of the material. Display is a right of the copyright holder. While a display to an individual is expected, display to a public group (a class) isn't. Material located shortly before use–before permission could normally be expected, say a week before anticipated use, since most webmasters can be reached electronically–could be used for a single lesson. Beyond that use, request permission. Any repeat use **always** needs permission, whether this re-use is in the same term or in subsequent terms.

Beware of programs that allow you to "capture" an entire Web site or portion of a site for use offline. While this is a boon to teachers with unreliable Web connections, downloading and storing Web pages or sites for public display in a classroom involve several problematic events. The author(s) and copyright holders design Web pages to be interactive and responsive. Many have ever-changing sponsorships and real-time data that is designed to be viewed in an active, not a static, environment. The owners of these sites have the authority to decide if they feel that your proposed collection of their work fits into their plans. Remember that under the fair use tests, one of the significant questions is how much of the item will be used. If one captures the entire site, one is taking 100 percent. Since Web pages are ordinarily highly creative in design and content (the character of the use), the likelihood for a ruling of fair use declines significantly.

In creating Web pages, one must have concerns about using copyrighted materials on those pages since the pages are distributed to the world. One must make copies to put a page on the Web, and frequently one must also convert materials from an analog format to digital to get the information on the Internet. Music, multimedia elements, and other copyrighted information, once mounted on a Web page, are not only copied but they are distributed and performed publicly. All these conditions are cause for concern. In the interest of copyright compliance, some rights brokers have established a "click-through" license for quick, efficient licensing (ASCAP, BMI). Note that there is no automatic fair use for these types of elements on open Web pages. Each individual use must be subjected to a fair use analysis.

Chat

Chat is as spontaneous as face-to-face conversation. However, few people record (or "fix") conversation. There is no case law regarding the ownership of chat conversations. Extrapolating from other media one might be able to say that chat is ephemeral, not being "fixed." In such a case, no copyright is vested in a communication that is not fixed in a tangible medium of expression. If the chat is captured, however, fixation automatically generates a copyright for the author of each communication. So each "send" might be construed as a separate "work" protected by copyright, or a series of posts might be taken as a long, possibly disjointed, document.

Blogs and Wikis

Both blogs and Wikis are "fixed" so they qualify for automatic copyright protection. The primary question is who owns the copyright? A single-author blog created by a teacher as part of his job (such as a librarian writing a book-review blog) would arguably be owned by the school district as work-for-hire. However, if the blog or Wiki were a shared work of students and faculty with the intention of creating a joint work, all the authors would share equally in the ownership of the combined work.

Copying Internet code

While it is possible to download a site's HTML code and adapt the design into your own page, remember that the creative work that went into the design is also copyrighted. Just as copying a drawing or painting requires permission, if you admire the design work of a Web page, ask the creator before you appropriate the result.

CHAPTER 10

Computer Software
in Schools

W hen the present version of the copyright law was adopted in 1976, computers were huge machines in refrigerated rooms. Few but the most visionary foresaw the emergence of computers as a household or personal appliance–certainly not the Congress as they moved through their deliberations. The 1976 copyright law offered protection to computer programs only as a new form of literary work. By 1980, however, computer programs received expanded protection under Section 117 of the newly revised statute. A revision of the law passed in 1992 brought software piracy to felony status, with fines up to $250,000 for systematic violations. The No Electronic Theft (NET) Act, passed in 1997, eliminated a loophole for those who provide infringing copies of software via the Internet and other networks. Those who willfully infringe over $2,500 worth of software are liable for infringement, whether or not a profit is made.

What typical activities are covered?

School personnel who knowingly lend computer software to persons who intend to copy it and school personnel who knowingly lend the necessary equipment to copy software may be charged with copyright infringement. This situation is known as contributory infringement. A school whose educators use software they know to be improperly made would be at risk of some sort of enforcement action.

Similarly, a principal who had been notified that an employee was violating copyright but who took no action could be charged with vicarious infringement if the employee knew the actions violated the law. One does not actually have to make the copy to be held liable. One must decide for oneself if the risk of suit is worth the activity.

Types of infringement

Infringement actions similar to those that can occur in the realm of print can also occur with computer software. The Software and Information Industry Association (SIIA) defines several types of software copying to which it objects. These types of copying would be ones that the SIIA would be willing to prosecute. Here are their definitions of the types of activities of which to be wary.

Direct infringement

"Anyone who violates any of the exclusive rights of the copyright owner [reproduction, adaptation, distribution to the public, public performance, public display, rental for commercial advantage or importation] is an infringer of the copyright or the right of the author" Section 501(a):

- downloading software
- uploading software
- making software available for download
- transmitting software files

Remember that you need not be the one actually making the illegal copies to be held liable for copyright infringement. Those who knowledgeably control the means necessary to make copies, or those who cause others to actually make the copies, are indirectly liable as well.

Indirect infringement

There are two types of indirect infringement: contributory infringement and vicarious liability. Both are possible in a school setting.

Contributory infringement

Anyone who knows or should have known that he or she is assisting, inducing, or materially contributing to infringement of any of the exclusive rights by another person is liable for contributory infringement. This includes:

- Posting of serial numbers.
- Posting of cracker utilities.
- Linking to FTP [file transfer protocol] sites where software may be unlawfully obtained.
- Informing others of FTP sites where software may be unlawfully obtained.
- Aiding others in locating or using unauthorized software.
- Supporting sites upon which the above information may be obtained.
- Allowing sites where the above information may be obtained to exist on a server.

Vicarious liability for infringement by another person

Anyone who has the authority and ability to control the actions of another person who infringes any of the exclusive rights, and who derives a financial benefit from the authority, is vicariously liable for the infringement of another person. Typical examples of vicarious liability would include:

- ISPs [Internet service providers] who have warez [proprietary software with copy protection removed illegally] or pirate sites on their system.
- ISPs who have pirates for customers.
- List owners for newsgroups or IRC [Internet Relay Chat] channels where pirate activity takes place. (Software and Information Industry Association, <http://siia.net/piracy/pubs/DirectIndirectCopyrightInfringement.pdf>)

 What rights are affected?

Computer software issues can affect virtually all of the rights reserved to the copyright holder:

- **Reproduction**: Copyright owners are especially concerned about reproduction of software because all copies are identical to the original. Software is expensive to develop, and each copy duplicated illegally is a significant amount of profit/cost recovery.

- **Adaptation**: Digital adaptation is easy and may be undetectable. Copyright owners worry about essential portions of their underlying code being stolen and reproduced in competition.

- **Distribution**: Distribution of software is fast, simple, and inexpensive compared to the costs involved in print distribution, for example. A digital work can be available around the world in a matter of seconds.

- **Public performance**: Performance of digital works can reduce demand for legitimate copies of the work.

- **Public display**: Public display is less possible for computer software, but digital images and other digital works such as Web pages are also displayed.

SPECIAL RULES THAT AFFECT COMPUTER SOFTWARE

Computer software is unique in many aspects. Because software is digital, copyright owners have developed different forms of distribution and different terms of sale than other, more traditional media. Software can be highly lucrative, and it begins at a high price point. As a result, software has suffered more piracy than most other media. Copyright owners responded with their own volleys, and the war was on. Various selling methods and distribution channels emerged to address these scuffles.

License vs. copyright

While most software (even "shareware") is copyrighted, the purchase of software is usually governed by a license agreement as well as by copyright law. The purchaser does not own the software, but rather the right to use the software in a manner described in a license agreement, usually included in the documentation of the software package. Reading and understanding the license agreement is an important part of acquiring a new package. Once accepted, these restrictions govern all use of the software.

There are several forms of license agreements:

- *Signed agreements:* The software includes a form that you must sign and return.

- *Some sort of warranty registration:* The software requires you to register in order to receive updates, or printer modifications, or other desirable benefits of registration. These types of licenses are a form of "click wrap" license (see shrink-wrap licenses).

- *Implied licenses:* Implied licenses are included in the software packaging, usually as a part of the documentation or as a separate sheet. These licenses usually say something like "use of the software after reading the license terms implies acceptance."

- *Shrink-wrap licenses:* Shrink-wrap licenses are often visible through a plastic overwrap on the software package. A similar type of license is called "click wrap" because the license appears when the software is installed. The user must click on an acknowledgment of the license to complete the software installation. The wording of both of these licenses will state that the user is bound by the conditions of the license if the shrink-wrap is opened or the accept button is clicked. If the signed license agreement is returned to the software company, or if you click on the "I agree" button, you will be legally bound by the restrictions imposed. This license agreement may supersede some standard rights under copyright, but it may also grant some extra privileges. Read the fine print to determine if you have permission to make any additional installations, and what permissions you may have.

- *Site license:* Some license agreements grant the purchaser the right to duplicate a specified number of copies–commonly called a limited site license. The software producer allows a discount on the software price, and in return the purchaser uses his own storage media and labor to make copies. Site licenses are generally specified on purchase orders, hence are legal and binding contracts between the purchaser and the producer.

Legitimate copying vs. piracy

Illegal copying of computer software is called "piracy." The rules on making copies of computer programs allow only two instances in which copies may be made of programs outside the scope of a valid license agreement:

1 A copy or adaptation may be made if such a copy is an essential part of the operation of the computer program. For example, if the program must be copied to the hard disk of the computer, that copying is acceptable. Since most, if not all, computer programs require the program to copy itself into the computer's memory in order to run, such an "ephemeral" copy is also permitted under this portion of the law. The program erases itself when the program is finished. In addition, modifications such as installing a printer driver or other customizations allowed by the software itself are also within the acceptable limits of adaptation.

2. A copy or adaptation for archival purposes may be made if the archival copy is not used. This copy can be on any storage medium, such as a CD or flash drive. The archival, or "backup" copy, should be destroyed if the program is sold or transferred. You may use the backup copy of the software and put the original away for safekeeping, or vice versa. Either is acceptable as long as both copies are not used at the same time. This provision is only for "owners" of software, however, not for licensees, so determine which you are before you make your backups.

Free software?

Two forms of software may be freely copied without any licenses or agreements. The first type is known as "public domain" software. Public domain software is a computer program that has been released by the author to be freely copied by whoever would like to use it. Such software is often found on Web sites dedicated to the public domain, and from computer users' groups and clubs. The title screen of the program or the documentation will indicate the public domain status of the program.

Another form of software that may be freely copied isn't exactly free. Known as "shareware," this software is copyright protected. The author or copyright holder has elected to distribute the software through a try-it-before-you-buy-it method. Shareware software is available through the same channels as public domain software; but once the software has been used and evaluated, the user is expected to register the software and pay a fee for the program. If users of shareware fail to register and pay for the software that they retain and use, this method of software distribution may disappear.

Open source software–software that is provided at no cost, but with strings on what you may do with the software or what you must do with any enhancements you might make to the software–may or may not be protected by copyright. Organizations such as the Creative Commons provide a variety of licenses that creators may apply to software. Licenses may allow you to freely use the software, or they may require that you freely share any development you make to the software. There are standard attribution requirements in using open source software, as well. Use caution in using some of the open source or freeware options such as Google Docs. The terms of service of some of these online services require that you relinquish your copyright in any documents that you upload! Always read the license and understand what you, your staff, and your students are giving up before you plan large use of such services.

Lending software

In 1990 Congress responded to the complaints of computer software producers that lending and renting of computer software were eroding the market for their products. The Copyright Software Rental Amendments Act was the result. In essence, the act granted to copyright owners (of computer software only) the right to control rental, lease, or lending of their software. However, the law did provide an exemption for nonprofit libraries provided that a specific warning of copyright is affixed to each package. This exemption for lending software is allowed for libraries only. Academic departments, administrators, or computer or technology directors may not make such loans because they do not qualify for this exemption.

Single-user programs

A common act of software piracy in schools is that of purchasing a single-user copy of a program and then installing it on multiple machines. Teachers and administrators rationalize the decision by saying that they aren't making any profit on the deal, and the school certainly can't afford all those single copies. Unfortunately, the end doesn't justify the means. Making copies worth more than $1,000 immediately raises the penalty for infringement to a criminal offense that can result in up to 10 years in prison plus associated fines (17 U.S.C. § 506, 18 U.S.C. § 2319).

If such multiple loads currently reside on programs in a district, often software producers will sell school districts licenses only for software at a greatly reduced price. The license includes no disks or documentation, but it legitimizes copies currently residing on the computers.

Networking

If the hardware will support it, network options allow multiple computers to share one copy of the software. However, networking software is not covered under fair use. All network and site licenses are contracts negotiated with the sellers–not a right under fair use. The fact that a particular piece of software can operate in a networked environment is immaterial. Networking a piece of computer software always requires a license.

Some software will permit unlimited networking within a single building. "Building" can be defined as an organizational campus–a group of students who have a separate administrative head. As long as those buildings comprise the physical plant of that organizational unit, any computer in those buildings could qualify to access a program under the network site license.

The software police

While the dreaded software police don't actually exist, the FBI can, and does, investigate and enforce suspected copyright violations as part of its general responsibilities. Since computer software piracy is now punishable as a felony (17 U.S.C. §§ 506), prosecution is pursued much more seriously. Schools and districts are advised by organizations such as the Business Software Alliance (BSA) and the Software and Information Industry Association (SIIA) to conduct software audits. Essentially this puts someone in the building–such as a librarian, technology director, or district administrator–and district in the position of software police. The SIIA even offers a school policy recommendation that outlines steps for maintaining records of legitimate copies of software. The SIIA also recommends several software programs that conduct a software audit by logging installed applications into a printed record. Vigorous application of a copyright compliance policy could subject employees to disciplinary procedures if they are found in violation of the copyright laws during such an audit.

Negotiated online database licenses are just as binding as computer software licenses. The databases may not be legally shared with other schools or to students at home if the license states "no remote access." This contract supersedes the Section 108 rights of libraries to provide information to anyone who requests it. In essence, by accepting the software license, the purchaser waives other rights under copyright, just as with regular computer software.

COPYRIGHT INFRINGEMENT VS. PLAGIARISM

A question arises concerning students who download or capture information from a database, CD-ROM, or other electronic sources. As in most student situations, students may use all sorts of information for personal research. The fact that the student has used electronic means to put the information into the product rather than hand-typing is irrelevant. The problem here is not copyright infringement, but plagiarism. The student may be operating within fair use to use the copyright protected materials, but his failure to cite the sources is plagiarism. For someone attempting to prove plagiarism, having information in electronic format is actually a blessing. The teacher need only do a simple text search of the source to find all instances of the wording in question.

In dealing with ethical issues such as copyright law compliance and plagiarism, it is important for administrators, teachers, and librarians to emphasize high expectations. Adherence to copyright law and rules against plagiarism should be fully detailed in student codes of conduct, with specific penalties for violations.

Software management tips

- Maintain copyright and license records on all programs in the building. If a site license or network copy was ordered, retain a copy of the purchase order as proof of the contract.

- Make one archival copy of each program and store it off-site. Do not use or circulate the archival copy. One archival copy of software documentation is allowed. More than one requires permission.

- Don't install non-network software on a network. Installing software on a network requires a network license.

- Don't lend equipment that would facilitate copying software. Don't own programs whose sole purpose is to "crack" software protection schemes.

- Refuse to lend software to library patrons who indicate they plan to make infringing copies. At minimum, inform them that the software is protected by copyright and their use of the software is governed by the notice affixed to the package.

- Place appropriate copyright warning stickers on all software circulated from the library.

- Register shareware.

- Enforce multi-user limitations. Install software metering programs or use network operating system security options to monitor licenses.

- Monitor use of computer scanners and digitizers. Encourage use of public domain and royalty-free graphics.

C H A P T E R **11**

Copyright Policies

Copyright policies are the skeleton that keeps your copyright compliance program together. A carefully worded, but not verbose, copyright policy states the expectation of the organization that the law be understood, obeyed, and enforced.

WHY HAVE ONE?

Why bother to have a copyright policy? There is no policy requiring compliance with the local building code, is there? Besides, who's going to catch a violator?

These questions are oversimplifying. Do police departments expect all motorists to observe the speed limit because it is the law? Hardly. That's why they purchase and use radar units. Publishers and media producers are of a similar opinion. They know people will attempt to violate their rights under copyright, and they exercise various means to discover and prosecute the offenders. And while an occasional inadvertent slip might be overlooked, widespread or systematic infringement is likely to bring a hailstorm of litigation.

The purpose of a copyright policy is to state the institution's intention to abide by the law. Association for Information Media and Equipment (AIME), the copyright watchdog group, boasts of its successes in redressing copyright infringement. While most of the cases are settled out of court, AIME publishes many of the settlements in its periodic newsletters. The majority of the settlements involve the establishment of an institutional policy regarding copyright as well as comprehensive training and plans for tracking and monitoring copyright compliance. Agreements to discharge key employees or place official letters of reprimand in personnel files are sometimes included in the out-of-court settlements.

Having an institutional copyright compliance policy is one way to beat the producers to the punch. AIME makes a good case with the following statement:

> AIME takes the position that a copyright policy is important for an educational entity to develop. It helps to avoid confusion on the part of the staff and administrators and takes a definitive position on the importance of knowing the law and obeying it. A copyright policy also has the potential to insulate the agency or institution and administrators from liability if an infringement action were to be instituted because of activities by individuals contrary to the policy and against the law" (Dohra, n.d.).

What should a policy contain?

AIME produces a packet of information on developing an institutional copyright policy. Included in the packet is a small booklet titled *A viewer's guide to copyright law: What every school, college and public library should know* (AIME, 1987). The primary author of this booklet is Ivan Bender, an attorney who specialized in copyright issues. The booklet has an excellent section on development of copyright policy.

Appendix F of this book is an example of a district-wide copyright policy. Several points in the policy are worth noting:

1. The policy states the institution's intention to abide by the letter and spirit of the copyright law and the associated congressional guidelines.

2. The policy covers all types of materials including print, nonprint, graphics, and computer software.

3. The liability for noncompliance with copyright rests with the individual using the work.

4. The district mandates training for all personnel who might need to make copies.

5. The person using the materials must be able to produce, on request, copyright justification for its use.

6. The district appoints a copyright officer who serves as a point of contact for copyright information both inside and outside the district. That person

will likely track licenses, serve as the registered copyright agent for the school's Web site, and oversee training of all students and teachers in copyright compliance.

Some authorities recommend additional measures be included in a policy, such as the assignment of a copyright officer, requiring the district to develop a copyright manual for all employees, requiring notices be affixed to all copy-capable equipment, and even reprinting the entire law and guidelines (Vleck, 1987, p. 10; AIME, 1987, p. 7).

Regardless of the wording of the policy, simply having a policy that states institutional intent to obey the law will provide some small measure of protection. However, the more the administrator and staff know about copyright and the management of copyrighted materials, the better protected the school district and its employees are from threat of suit. If an infringement were to occur, the administration that has undertaken a thorough copyright education program could present a credible case that they did not condone the activity and that they had taken vigorous action to prevent infringement. The infringing employee, though, would have a poor chance of claiming "innocent infringement," because the institution would have records of staff development in correct application of copyright principles.

A further measure to protect the institution from individual acts of infringement is to have employees sign a statement indicating they have been informed of copyright laws and guidelines and that they will abide by both the institutional policy and the applicable laws. (See Appendix A.) This is similar to the OSHA requirement that employees be informed of hazards of chemicals in the workplace. Frequently employees are required to view a training tape or attend a staff development session on a topic for which they are "signed off." Such record-keeping indemnifies the organization from claims of negligence in informing the employees of potential hazards.

The most efficient way to develop a copyright policy is to search out examples of model policies. AIME provides multiple examples of acceptable policies in its copyright policy development kit <http://www.aime.org/products.php>. A custom-developed copyright policy can be quickly assembled by cutting and pasting the best parts of the samples. Administrators, librarians, television, and media people should all have a say in the final wording. Bringing in an outside expert may be the best way to persuade doubters who believe a comprehensive policy isn't necessary. The final draft of the policy should go to the district's legal counsel for approval, because collective bargaining agreements and teacher contracts may affect wording of policies. A spokesperson should be prepared to appear before the board to underscore the importance of the policy and explain the risk of leaving copyright compliance to individual employees. And a plan should be in place to train employees and monitor compliance in libraries, classrooms, and offices.

CHAPTER 12

Appendices

APPENDIX A

COPYRIGHT COMPLIANCE AGREEMENT

MIDDLETOWN SCHOOL DISTRICT

COPYRIGHT
COMPLIANCE AGREEMENT

I have been informed of the appropriate uses of instructional media, fair use guidelines, and the copyright compliance policy of the Middletown School District. I, the undersigned, acknowledge that I understand these policies and guidelines and that any uses I may make of instructional materials or audiovisual equipment in a classroom setting will be in accordance with both federal law and said policies and guidelines.

_____
Teacher

_____
Date

_____
Campus

APPENDIX B

COPYRIGHT DO's *and* DON'TS
for SCHOOLS

Do make sure that all audiovisual material shown to students is directly related to the curriculum. Be especially aware of film ratings (G, PG, R) since an inappropriate film won't meet the instructional requirement of fair use.

Don't show films or videos for reinforcement or reward. Encourage teachers to try popcorn and coke parties, games, stickers, or free time. You may rent movies for such performances, paying a minimal public performance fee, from suppliers such as Movie Licensing USA. Video rental stores cannot authorize you to give public performances.

Do ask your faculty to sign a copyright compliance agreement.

Don't loan VCRs or DVD-Rs with patch cords. Watch for questionable situations: Why would a teacher need two recorders except to copy programs?

Do write the record date on all videos you record.

Do write the required erase date on all videos you record. This date will vary with the program. See advertisement of program, flyer from producer, or calculate fair use date.

Don't copy commercial computer software, except to make an archival (one that isn't used) copy.

Don't copy cartoon or TV or film characters for decorations, bulletin boards, or handouts. Purchasing clip art, duplicator books, and bulletin board figures is acceptable, but you may not enlarge, modify, or change the medium (e.g., make slides or coloring sheets).

Do keep receipts and purchase orders for all videos and computer software. Keep the catalog (or pertinent pages) to verify purchase of public performance rights.

Do require teachers to verify recording date and source for all home-recorded videos. Fair use guidelines say that programs must be used for classroom instruction within 10 days of taping. After that date, the recording may only be used for evaluation for possible purchase. Erase after 45 days.

Do write for permission to retain recordings of useful programs. The worst a copyright holder can do is say no.

Don't record programs off cable without investigating the recording rights first. Only programs recorded off the air (VHF and UHF channels) can be recorded without express permission. Look for this permission in teacher's guides that the various networks and program producers send out. These guides will also tell you the retention rights (e.g., seven days plus fair use; one year; life of tape/disc). Keep a photocopy of the permission with the recording at all times, and make sure there is a copyright notice on each copy.

Do post a copyright notice on VCRs, DVRs, scanners, computers, overhead projectors, and opaque projectors similar to that on your photocopy machine.

Don't record a program because you know a teacher will ask for it later. Requests to record programs must come from a teacher in advance and in writing. Also, requests to record programs must come from the "bottom up," i.e., your teachers can ask you to record programs, but your principal may not.

Do remember that the person who pushes the button is also liable. So is the principal who knows copyright is being violated. We recommend you notify in writing both the principal and teacher when you are aware of copyright infringement. Keep a copy in your own file.

Do keep a link to Kidsnet (<kidsnet.org>) or Cable in the Classroom Online (<www.ciconline.org>) to verify taping rights from the various networks. Kidsnet also lists supporting materials and addresses where inexpensive copies of non-recordable programs can be obtained.

Do encourage teachers to use fast forward. Often only a portion of a video will make as effective a point as an entire film. Also, some producers will allow use of "excerpts" when they will not allow use of an entire program. Write for permission.

Don't create anthologies on tape, disc, or the photocopier. Copying an article, poem, or excerpt is fine, but combining them into a "new work" is not permitted.

Don't apologize for obeying federal law. If you would like a free copy of the law, visit the Copyright Office Web site for a copy of Circular 92.

APPENDIX C

COPYRIGHT WARNING NOTICES

All interlibrary loan (ILL) request forms must include the following notice (Code of Federal Regulations, Title 37, Section 201.14). It must be printed within a prominent box on the actual order form. The notice may be on the front of the form, or adjacent to the section requiring the patron's signature. The notice cannot be in type any smaller than that used throughout the form, and in no case may it be smaller than 8-point type. The notice must be clearly apparent, legible, and comprehensible to even a casual viewer of the form. Standard ALA ILL forms available from library supply houses comply with this requirement.

The same notice must be displayed at the place where ILL orders are taken. Such notice must be printed on heavy paper, in type no less than 18 points in size. It must be placed so as to be clearly visible, legible and comprehensible near the place where ILL orders are accepted.

NOTICE WARNING CONCERNING COPYRIGHT RESTRICTIONS

The copyright law of the United States (Title 17, United States Code) governs the making of photocopies or other reproductions of copyrighted material. Under certain conditions specified in the law, libraries and archives are authorized to furnish a photocopy or other reproduction. One of these specific conditions is that the photocopy or reproduction is not to be "used for any purpose other than private study, scholarship, or research." If a user makes a request for, or later uses, a photocopy or reproduction for purposes in excess of "fair use," that user may be liable for copyright infringement. This institution reserves the right to refuse to accept a copying order if, in its judgment, fulfillment of the order would involve violation of copyright law.

Photocopies made by libraries, both for interlibrary loan and for patrons, should be marked with a copy if all information from the original copyright notice, or the copyright page copied and included with the item. If an item has no copyright notice, a notice of possible copyright restrictions must be added. While specific wording isn't detailed in the law, many libraries use wording similar to the following:

The multimedia guidelines specify that a notice must be on the opening slide (not necessarily the title slide) of a work that incorporates copyright protected materials. The wording is not specified in the guidelines though the content of the notice is described. Adults may use a notice similar to this:

Young students must also have a compliant notice on their presentations. A notice that a young student might be able to understand, yet still meeting the intent of the guidelines, would be:

Software circulated by nonprofit libraries must have the following notice "durably attached" to each package:

Appendix D

SAMPLE COPYRIGHT POLICY

It is the intent of the XYZ School District, its board of trustees, staff, and students, to adhere to the provisions of current copyright laws and Congressional guidelines. Employees and students are to adhere to all provisions of Title 17 of the United States Code, entitled "Copyrights," and other relative federal legislation and guidelines related to the duplication, retention, and use of copyrighted materials.

Specifically:

- Unlawful copies of copyrighted materials may not be produced on district-owned equipment.

- Unlawful copies of copyrighted material may not be used with district-owned equipment, within district-owned facilities, or at district-sponsored functions.

- The legal and insurance protection of the district will not be extended to employees who intentionally and unlawfully copy and use copyrighted materials.

- Employees who make copies and/or use copyrighted materials in their jobs are expected to be familiar with published provisions regarding fair use and public display, and are further expected to be able to provide their supervisor, upon request, the justification under sections 107 or 110 of U.S.C. 17 for materials that have been used or copied.

Employees who use copyrighted materials that do not fall within fair use or public display guidelines will be able to substantiate that the materials meet the following tests:

- The materials have been purchased from an authorized vendor by the individual or the district and a record of the purchase exists.

- The materials are copies covered by a licensing agreement between the copyright owner and the district or the individual employee, OR;

- The materials are being previewed or demonstrated by the user to reach a decision about future purchase or licensing and a valid agreement exists that allows for such use.

- The district will appoint an officer to assist employees in fulfilling their obligations under U.S. Copyright law, and who will maintain records of licenses and permissions.

APPENDIX E

MIDDLETOWN SCHOOL DISTRICT
PUBLICATION RELEASE FORM

I, the undersigned, having full authority to execute this Release on behalf of myself and on behalf of _____(child's name) of _____ (school name) hereby grant permission to MIDDLETOWN SCHOOL DISTRICT (hereinafter called "MSD") to use the following materials provided by me or on my child's behalf to MSD, for the purposes identified below:

My or my child's: (initial where appropriate)

Name _____ Voice _____ Likeness _____ Quotes

_____ Papers, articles, poems or other written material as specified:

_____

_____

_____

_____Graphics, photographs, or other artwork as specified:

_____

_____

_____

I warrant and represent that the materials submitted under this agreement are owned by and/or are original to me or my child, and/or I have full authority from the owner of said materials to permit MSD to use said materials in the manner described below (initial as appropriate):

_____ Newspapers, magazines, other print publications

_____ Television or radio _____ Internet or computer network

_____ Presentation for teaching, staff development or professional conference

_____ Retention and use as exemplars _____ Public display or performance.

I understand that MSD is and shall be the exclusive owner of any and all right, title, and interest, including copyright, to any and all materials into which the aforementioned items are incorporated, except as to my preexisting rights in any of the items herein released.

_____
Signature   Date

_____
Name/Relationship

_____
Address

_____
Telephone

APPENDIX F

COPYRIGHT *and* PLAGIARISM GUIDELINES *for* STUDENTS

1. You may make a single photocopy of any material you need to do your schoolwork, or for your own personal research. You may keep the copies you make as long as you like, but you may not sell them, nor may you make copies of your copies.

2. You must respect the copyright of the materials you use. Only the creators, or the persons or companies who own the copyright may make copies of the material, except as noted above. You may not modify or change the material, nor may you perform or display the material except in conjunction with class work.

3. You may use copyrighted material to do your schoolwork, but if you use an author's ideas you must give the author credit, either in the text or in a footnote. If you use an author's words, you must put the words in quotation marks or other indication of direct quotation. Failure to give credit to the author is plagiarism. If you use an extensive amount of a single work, you must obtain permission.

4. Use of copyrighted materials outside of regular class work requires written permission of the copyright holder. This includes graphic material such as cartoon characters on posters or other spirit or decorative matter.

5. You may not copy computer software from the school computers.

6. Information received from the school computers may be used only for regular schoolwork or personal research.

7. The source of any information used in your school work should be acknowledged in the format prescribed by the teacher. Use of another's intellectual work without attribution is plagiarism, as outlined in the Student Code of Conduct.

APPENDIX G

IMPORTANT INTERNET LINKS *for* COPYRIGHT INFORMATION

Agreement on Guidelines for Classroom Copying in Not-For-Profit Educational Institutions with Respect to Books and Periodicals <http://www.lib.jmu.edu/org/mla/Guidelines/Accepted%20Guidelines/Educational%20Photocopying.aspx>

American Library Association. Copyright and fair use. <http://www.ala.org/ala/alcts/divgroups/ig/nrm/copyrightfair.cfm>

Association for Instructional Media and Equipment <http://www.aime.org/>

Brad Templeton's "10 Big Myths about Copyright Explained" <http://www.templetons.com/brad/copymyths.html>

Complying with the Digital Millennium Copyright Act <http://www.utsystem.edu/OGC/IntellectualProperty/dmcaisp.htm>

Copyright Condensed. Heartland Area Education Agency <http://www.aca11.k12.ia.us/help/copyright.pdf>

Copyright for educators <http://falcon.jmu.edu/~ramseyil/copy.htm>

Copyright for music librarians <http://www.lib.jmu.edu/org/mla/>

Copyright resources for schools and libraries. Wisconsin Dept. of Public Instruction <http://www.dpi.state.wi.us/dpi/dltcl/lbstat/copyres.html>

Copyright Law in Cyberspace <http://www.utsystem.edu/OGC/IntellectualProperty/distance.htm>

Copyright Notices for Supervised Library Copying: Updated Information for Library Services <http://www.copyright.iupui.edu/super_copying.htm>

Copyright Office. Online Service Providers <http://www.copyright.gov/onlinesp/>

Copyright Timeline <http://www.arl.org/pp/ppcopyright/copyresources/copytimeline.shtml>

Copyright Web site <http://www.benedict.com>

Copyright workshop <http://www.cyberbee.com/copyrt.html>

Designation of Copyright Agent, Library of Congress <http://www.copyright.gov/onlinesp/>

Fair Use Guidelines for Educational Multimedia <http://www.utsystem.edu/ogc/intellectualproperty/ccmcguid.htm>

Guidelines for Educational Uses of Music
<http://www.lib.jmu.edu/org/mla/Guidelines/Other%20Guidelines/
Educational%20Use%20of%20Music.aspx>

Guidelines for Off-Air Recordings of Broadcast Programming
for Educational Purposes
<http://www.lib.jmu.edu/org/mla/Guidelines/Accepted%20Guidelines/
Off-Air%20Recording.aspx>

Library and Classroom Use of Copyrighted Videotapes and Computer Software
<http://www.ifla.org/documents/infopol/copyright/ala-1.txt>

MARC record guidelines for copyright management information
<http://lcweb.loc.gov/marc/bibliographic/ecbdnot2.html#mrcb540>

PBS Teacher Source
<http://www.pbs.org/teachersource/copyright/copyright.shtm>

PDInfo–Public Domain Music <http://www.pdinfo.com/>

Performance Rights for Copyrighted Videorecordings
<http://dpi.wi.gov/lbstat/coplicen.html >

Public Domain Report <http://www.publicdomain.org>

Report on Copyright and Digital Distance Education (U.S. Copyright Office)
<http://www.copyright.gov/disted>

Sample off-air videotape label
<http://web.archive.org/web/20050516235507/http://www.pbs.org/teacher-
source/copyright/copyright_sample_label.shtm>

Software and Information Industry Association. Software Use & the Law
<http://www.siia.net/piracy/pubs/SoftwareUseLaw.pdf>

Stanford University. Copyright and Fair Use Web site
<http://fairuse.stanford.edu/>

University of Texas System Crash Course on Copyright
<http://www.utsystem.edu/ogc/intellectualproperty/cprtindx.htm>

Use of Music on a Multimedia Web site
<http://www.ivanhoffman.com/music.html>

Using Software: A Guide to the Ethical and Legal Use of Software for Members
of the Academic Community
<http://www.ifla.org/documents/infopol/copyright/educom.txt>

A Visit to Copyright Bay <http://www.stfrancis.edu/cid/copyrightbay/>

World Book and Copyright Day – UNESCO <www.unesco.org/culture/bookday/>

APPENDIX H

COPYRIGHT INFRIGEMENT FORM
MIDDLETOWN SCHOOL DISTRICT

MSD has the legal responsibility to abide by copyright laws. Employees of the District shall comply with all provisions of United States Copyright Law. Board Policies outline the District's copyright policy.

Name of Person(s) Allegedly Violating Copyright Laws

_____

_____

Campus _____

Date of Infringement _____

Describe exactly what happened. Be sure to include what items were infringed, where it happened, and how many times it happened.

_____

_____

_____

_____

_____

_____

_____

_____

_____

_____

Person making report (optional) _____

Please return this form to the district copyright officer

WORKS CITED

Althouse, J. (1997). Copyright: the complete guide for music educators. (2d ed.).
Van Nuys, CA: Alfred.

Association for Information Media and Equipment. (1987). A viewer's guide to
copyright law: what every school, college, and public library should know.
Elkader, IA: AIME.

Association for Information Media and Equipment. 1990. Press release. Elkader,
IA: AIME.

Band, Jonathan. (2001) The Digital Millennium Copyright Act. Washington, D.C.:
Association of Research Libraries. Retrieved July 14, 2007 from
<http://www.arl.org/info/frn/copy/band.html>.

Bender, I. (1996). The Internet–It's not free and never was. AIME News. Summer,
1996.

Blair, Julie. (1998). "Pirated Software Could Prove Costly to L.A. District."
Education Week. Vol. 17 Issue 43. Aug 1998: 3, 2/5

Business Software Alliance. (24 February 1999). Five Southern California
Organizations Settle Software Copyright Claims. Retrieved July 14, 2007
from <http://www.bsa.org/usa/press/newsreleases/Five-Southern-California-
Organizations-Settle-Software-Copyright-Claims.cfm>.

Business Software Alliance. (24 February 1999). Five Southern California
Organizations Settle Software Copyright Claims. Retrieved January 5, 2004
from <http://www.bsa.org/usa/press/newsreleases/Five-Southern-California-
Organizations-Settle-Software-Copyright-Claims.cfm>.

Clean Flicks v. Soderbergh, 433 F.Supp.2d 1236 (D.Colo. 2005)

Complying with the Digital Millennium Copyright Act and Sonny Bono
Copyright Term Extension Act. (2001).
<http://www.utsystem.edu/ogc/INTELLECTUALPROPERTY/dmcalib.htm>

Crews, Kenneth. 1998. Bloomington, IN: Indiana University Online Copyright
Tutorial.

Dohra, A. (n.d.). Copyright information packet. Elkader, IA: AIME.

Educational Multimedia Fair Use Guidelines Development Committee. (1997).
<http://www.utsystem.edu/OGC/IntellectualProperty/ccmcguid.htm>

Eldred v. Ashcroft, 537 U.S. 186, (2003).

Hoffman, I. (2002). The visual artists rights act.
<http://www.ivanhoffman.com/vara.html>.

Hutchins, Pat. Rosie's Walk. Aladdin, 1971.

I.T. Vibe. (1 May 2004). RIAA sue another 477 music sharers.
<http://itvibe.com/news/2501/>

Individuals with Disabilities Education Improvement Act of 2004, PL 108-446, December 3, 2004, 118 Stat 2647 (2005).

Jensen, M.B. (1992, Winter). I'm not my brother's keeper: Why libraries shouldn't worry too much about what patrons do with library materials at home. The Bookmark, 50, 150-4.

Kelly v. Arriba Soft Corp., 280 F.3d 937 (9th Cir. 2002).

Lutzker, Arnold. (1999). Memorandum.
<http://www.arl.org/info/frn/copy/notice.html>.

Making Digital Copies in the Library. (2001).
<http://www.utsystem.edu/ogc/INTELLECTUALPROPERTY/dmcalib.htm>

Music Publisher's Association. (2004). Making a Record: Do I Have To Obtain a Mechanical License? <http://www.mpa.org/copyright/you.html#record>

Office of General Counsel, University of Texas System. (2004, December 22). CONFU: the Conference on Fair Use.
<http://www.utsystem.edu/OGC/IntellectualProperty/confu.htm>

Reed, M. H. 1989. Videotapes: copyright and licensing considerations for schools and libraries. Syracuse, NY: ERIC Clearinghouse on Information Resources. (ERIC Document Reproduction Service No. ED 308 855).

Sinofsky, E. (14 June 1993). Re: Closed-caption videotape conversion. Discussion on the addition of closed captioning to commercial videotapes. Message posted to CNI-COPYRIGHT electronic mailing list.

Special Interest Video Sales Group. 1995. Fair use doctrine.
<http://www.sivideo.com/9fstsleb.htm>

UCLA Online Institute for Cyberspace Law and Policy. (1998). The 'No Electronic Theft' Act. July 14, 2007 from
<http://www.gseis.ucla.edu/iclp/hr2265.html>.

United States Department of Justice. (1997). Criminal Resource Manual 1844 Copyright Law–Preemption of State Law.
<http://www.usdoj.gov/usao/eousa/foia_reading_room/usam/title9/crm01844.htm>.

United States Department of Justice. (1998). The 'No Electronic Theft' Act.
<http://www.cybercrime.gov/netsum.htm>

Vleck, C.W. (1987). Copyright policy development: a resource book for educators. Friday Harbor, WA: Copyright Information Services.

INDEX

A

A&M Records, Inc. v. Napster, Inc., 284 F.3d 1091 (C.A.9 (Cal.), 2002)., 59

Access Learning Magazine, 52

 taping rights, 102

adaptation

 audiovisual materials, 48

 definition, 2

 digital video, 57

 disability accommodations, 40

 expurgate (censor offensive materials), 48

 format changes, 2

 illustrations, 39

 print materials, 36

 scanning graphics, 43

 sheet music, 62

 transferring the work to another medium, 51

AIME. See Association for Information Media and Equipment (AIME)

American Library Association (ALA)

 interlibrary loan forms, 104

American Printing House for the Blind, 40

American Society of Composers, Authors & Publishers (ASCAP), 59, 66, 83

answer sheets. See consumable materials

anthologies, 102

 creation of, 63, 70

 creation of (educational use), 62

 creation of (film), 48, 51

 guidelines, 37

 music, 63

 poetry, 70

 substitution for, 42

archival copies

 audiovisual materials, 56

 computer software, 55

E

educational institutions
    definition, 68
educational multimedia projects
    definition, 68
educational purposes
    definition, 68
Eldred v. Ashcroft, 537 U.S. 186, 2003, 10
e-mail. See Internet Services
ERIC, 41
essence of the work
    definition, 28
ethical issues, 16, 92
exemptions, 31, 40, 46, 48, 62, 65, 66, 76
    library, 31
    school, 30
expurgate (censor offensive materials), 48

F

face-to-face teaching, 64
    activities, 49, 50, 65
facts, 6, 19, 27
    charts of measures, 6
    creative expression, 27
    links, individual, 78
    multiplication tables, 6
fair use, 29
    brevity, 33
    burden of proof, 24
    cumulative effect, 33
    definition, 24
    exemptions, 23, 31, 55, 70, 105
    impact on market for (value of) a work, 28–29
    limits on educational use See also Kastenmeier report, 36
    misconceptions, 24
    Section 107 (overview), 33
    spontaneity, 33
fair use assessment
    "four tests", 23, 24, 25, 79, 80, 82

fair use overview

    market value, effect of use on, 23, 24

    nature of the work, 23, 24

    purpose and character of use, 23, 24

    substantiality, 23, 24

film. See videos

First Amendment right to free speech, 24

forms

    copyright infringement reporting, 116

    ILL form and notice of copyright restrictions, 104

    student work release form, 109

four tests of fair use. See fair use assessment:"four tests"

FTP. See Internet services: file transfer protocol

G

general cultural value, 50

government documents

    authored by federal employees, 19

    public domain, 6, 19

graphic novels, 39

graphics, 42

    adaptation, 42

    print fair use guidelines, 42

    thumbnail images, 27

guidelines

    audiovisual materials, 46

    copyright and plagarism, 111

Guidelines for Educational Uses of Music, 62, 63

H

handicapped. See disability accommodations

Harry Fox Agency, 66

House Judiciary Subcommittee, 36

I

infringement

    action against schools, 16

    Congressional Guidelines (benchmark), 33

    contributory, 13

    contributory (definition), 57

L

M

MARC record
>guidelines Web site, 114

moral rights, 5

Movie Licensing USA, 51

MP3 files. See digital audio recordings

multimedia materials
>copying, 70
>definition, 68
>network access, 69
>notice of copyright, 70
>notice of copyright (sample), 70
>quantity limits, 69
>retention, 69

music
>background, 58, 65
>digital sound recordings, 4
>emergency copies, 63

Music Publisher's Association, 66

N

National Technical Institute for the Deaf, 56

NET Theft ("No Electronic Theft") Act
>criminal penalties, 59

NET Theft ("No Electronic Theft") Act, 8, 9, 85

network security, 75
>access, 91

newsgroup. See Internet services

newsletters, 3, 36, 94

No Electronic Theft (NET) Act (P.L. 105-147), 58

nonprofit educational, 80

notice of copyright
>print copies, 38

notices of copyright, 103–5
>audiovisual materials, 75
>computer software, 90, 92
>copy-capable equipment, 95
>music, 63
>networked multimedia, 69

teachers

　　documentation (audiovisual materials), 57

Technology, Education And Copyright Harmonization Act. See TEACH
　Act (Technology, Education And Copyright Harmonization Act)

television

　　broadcast channels, 52

　　broadcast programming off-air recording, 52

　　educators' guides, 52

　　home taping, 54

　　off-air recording of rebroadcasts, 53

　　off-air videotape copies, 54

　　off-air videotape retention, 53

　　programming taping rights, 102

　　satellite programming, 52

　　taping in anticipation, 54

television transmissions

　　broadcast, cable, and satellite, 47

templates. See consumable materials

Title 17, United States Code, Public Law 94-553, 90 Stat. 2541, 1

　　Circular 92 (free copy of the law), 102

training

　　copyright education program, 95

　　copyright officer, 94

　　mandated, 94

　　staff development session, 95

transparency, 80

U

umbrella licenses. See license: umbrella licenses

unpublished materials, 8

V

video distribution systems, 3, 48, 57

　　definition, 56

videos

　　digital format (cartoon), 2

　　home use only, 51

　　piracy, 15

　　public performance restrictions, 50

　　use logs, 53

W

warez (illegal software sites), 87

Washington, George (President), 1

Web pages, 81, 82

      public display (classroom), 82

      scanned materials, 4

      source code, 83

work for hire, 7

workbooks. See consumable materials

worksheets. See consumable materials